P9-BUI-474
Sincerely

FROM PULPIT TO PRISON

FROM PULPIT TO PRISON

A Clergyman's fight for justice

THE REVEREND RUSSELL D. HORSBURGH

Methuen
TORONTO LONDON SYDNEY WELLINGTON

Library of Congress Catalog Card Number 77-101155
SBN 458 90510 0

Printed and bound in Canada
1 2 3 4 5 73 72 71 70 69

TO CHATHAM, WITH LOVE

CONTENTS

FOREWORD / ix
PREFACE / xx
PART 1
THE PHILOSOPHY BEHIND MY MINISTRY / 3
Chapter 1 / 5
Chapter 2 / 12
Chapter 3 / 27
PART 2
OPERATION CHATHAM / 33
Chapter 4 / 35
Chapter 5 / 41
Chapter 6 / 50
Chapter 7 / 58
Chapter 8 / 61
Chapter 9 / 65
Chapter 10 / 69
Chapter 11 / 83
Chapter 12 / 88
Chapter 13 / 114
Chapter 14 / 117
Chapter 15 / 126
PART 3
WHERE DO I GO FROM HERE? / 129
Chapter 16 / 131
Chapter 17 / 143
EPILOGUE / 147

FOREWORD

About eight years ago I received an invitation to deliver the Sunday lecture-sermon in a forum series being presented in a church in Chatham, Ontario. The bid to occupy a Christian pulpit was no longer a novelty: exchange between Protestant pastor and rabbi had become a Brotherhood Week routine. But it was Lent – and my subject was "A Jewish View of the Crucifixion" – a subject suggested by the church's minister, who urged me to take off the kid gloves.

In any Canadian church such an invitation would have been a prelude to raised eyebrows and raised blood-pressure. In the conservative bastion of Chatham, it invited schism and possible disaster. . . .

The author of that daring and provocative proposal was Russell Horsburgh. As I had already preached for him on the same subject (during Lent) at his former church in Waterloo, and as I remembered him as a man of rare intellectual integrity and moral courage, I accepted.

So far as I could learn, my uninhibited evaluation of the Crucifixion as dubious history and as the seed-bed of historic anti-Semitism did not spark an immediate storm of wrath around the minister's head, although all the courtesy and restraint in that good Christian audience could not conceal its dismay.

After the service, Russell Horsburgh and I had a leisurely chat in his study. He had come to the Chatham parish only a few months before and seemed eager to talk about his plans. Among the projects that he outlined – with warm enthusiasm – was a lecture-discussion course on sex, directed particularly at the young.

I listened to the glowing prospectus with mounting astonishment. What naïvete! Suicidal! That eager stalwart of open windows and the open mind was newly arrived, without time to establish roots, make friends, marshal allies. Yet, he would plunge into the most provocative and perilous of all arenas of public discourse. Sex had been barred from the schools. In all likelihood it was taboo as a subject of discourse (and a breeder of "original-sin" guilt-feelings in intercourse, even in the marital bed) for most of his congregants. "The birds and the bees" were still, I suspected, the stammering and embarrassed staple of Chatham parents goaded into "sex-education" by their children. And here a pastor was bent on lugging the inflammable topic into the sanctuary!

The naïvete Russell Horsburgh revealed that day, in my judgment, was the inner lash that drove him from pulpit to prison. He believed that sincerity, forthrightness, and passion for truth would gird any cause in steel-plated armor against narrow perspectives, pettifogging fear of revolutionary change, self-righteousness (most baleful of all the fruits of organized-religion respectability) and the ambivalent criticism of ecclesiastical colleagues who had to condemn his dangerous folly while (at least in some cases) secretly envying his courage. . . .

He believed that steadily-accruing clerical authority over young chaos could be garnered by meeting potential or active delinquents on their own terms within the revered domain of the church (although they no longer revered it). He began by offering them limited latitude (which was interpreted, apparently, to mean participatory license), and by risking his career in an unreserved gesture of trust in youngsters who, despite his "good fellow" image (always a snare to the clergy), never really forgave him for being a "square". They turned upon him as the embodiment of the institutionalized religious establishment they inarticulately and perhaps even unknowingly despised, and may have taken perverse pleasure in making him the scapegoat and stimulant of their depravity. (Also, Horsburgh made the grave practical error of placing himself in the hands of persons so young they could disclaim responsibility – or suspect they had nothing to lose by so doing.)

The romantic unrealism of Russell Horsburgh, however, merely added a special depth-dimension to his difficulty. Assuming that his life-style had as its central pattern and objective the unswerving leadership of his flock into new insights and fresh, enlightened attitudes toward ideas and people, it was doomed to founder on the paradox that hems in and can destroy all but a few rare charismatic clergymen. That paradox is stark and simple: the preacher, like the politician, is dependent, for career, status, identity – and, more likely in the preacher's case, for elementary livelihood – on the suffrage and sufferance of those who presumably submit themselves to him for guidance. Before he is permitted to lose himself in the service of God, he must win the support of men (and perhaps even more, of women). In this respect, he resembles the commanding officer of an army unit who can be hired and fired by his men!

It is not the nature of the human animal to embrace "new insights and fresh enlightened attitudes". He is a stubborn advocate of what is; the mere mention of what should be can frighten and antagonize him. Change is the enemy of habit, cerebral indolence, contentment: universal attributes of mankind, notably of that (dwindling?) segment that sits regularly, rigidly, and respectably in the pews of church and synagogue. When a radical violates peace in the streets, society pays the police to suppress him. When a radical violates peace of mind (namely, complacency) in the pulpit, the congregation pays *him*! Trustees, elders, members of church and synagogue would not verbalize such an illogical and contradictory situation – but when their "spiritual leader" ventures into questionable areas of thought and deed, they show sensitive awareness of its cost.

Because the average man has allowed his capacity for independent thinking to be atrophied by disuse, and whereas conformity tends to become the prime social virtue in a technological mass-communication age, the mere fact of individual judgment is an act of dissent. Of all the repositories of tradition and the way things have been, formal religion is the most hallowed and conservative. Even those religions that began with a bang of rebellion against ankylosis of the spiritual and intellectual joints crystallize into creeds, canons, and the "right thing," and may deteriorate into a prolonged burp, with an occasional whimper of social protest for a placebo.

The founder of a dissenting religious movement may be its last dissenter. And the anti-Horsburgh faction in the Chatham church may have recalled that Martin Luther combined rebellion against Rome with social and political reaction. (They surely did not remember his alleged bowel-obsession.)

Yet, their pastor, ostensibly a paragon of propriety, dared to hew out untried paths in the dark jungle of sex-behavior over which the Sunday-School text-books have tacked the label "Morality".

In the listing of qualifications for Divine favor, preservation of "virtue," otherwise known as sexual purity, retains to this day the top-priority status accorded it in ancient scriptures of all faiths, particularly in the Christian Bible. The long historic process whereby perforation of the hymen or frenetic friction of the epidermis became a gate to hell is probably the most fascinating and mysterious stage in the emergence and growth of human self-discipline. But it has bred such an imbalance of values that a man may be an ogre in business, cruel and callous in all human relationships, and yet a likely candidate for salvation if he has never bedded with anyone save his lawful wedded wife. And this pivotal concern with the sheer physical act of sex has inflated the private sex-life of the clergyman into a matter of congregational concern potentially so obsessive that it can preempt and poison his total relationship to his people. . . . Once Russell Horsburgh's "morals" began to be talked about, his usefulness as a minister began to end, and, one after another, doors opened in the service of God and man – however fruitfully and sacrificially he had labored to open them – began to close. The church's prime role is guardian of the moral code; the minister, guardian of the church, must be impeccable!

The context of Divine partnership in which a clergyman is viewed, especially by avid female devotees of the faith, surrounds him in an emotional aura, a poetic, other-worldly afflatus that sets him apart from other men – and yet he is a man, all the more vulnerable, perhaps, because he unconsciously dramatizes the troubled union of flesh and spirit. (The self-revelations of mediaeval mystics, great preachers, and pre-Graham evangelists hint at a link between God-intoxication, spiritual vitality, and erotic imagination.) And a cleric's "cool" is not hardened by the stewardship to which the cloth calls him, namely, responsibility for the preservation, intact, of a code of chastity increasingly dubbed irrelevant, abnormal, and psychologically harmful, dismissed with hardly a shrug by an alarming proportion of the young, undermined by much that passes for entertainment and culture in our permissive, sex-ridden age, and deprived of its supernatural authority by the breakdown of belief in divinely-ordained Law (a trauma from which some clergymen themselves have not been able to escape).

The Horsburgh "scandal" deviated from the normal pattern. Alleged sinning by church dignitaries usually meant clandestine adultery, occasional molestation of minors, or a comparatively rare charge of incitement to homosexuality. The accusations against Russell Horsburgh, now discredited and erased by the Supreme Court of Canada (and, therefore, I believe no longer a basis for further inaction by the United Church of Canada), were spawned by an officially planned, publicly announced, and openly (if unwisely) implemented program of education he projected as leader and teacher of his flock. It was not furtive fumbling under a chorister's robe, a kiss in the dark corner of the church house, or a pastoral call on a neurotic housewife.

That very forthrightness of Horsburgh's frontal attack on "respectability" doomed him. The keepers of the gods can forgive hidden infractions against sacred mores. Indeed, peccadillos committed under concealing wraps are a kind of tribute to the punitive power of established authority – and the wrong-doers may even be treated with some sympathy and condescension as human beings subject to universal human frailty and no less capable of regeneration than St. Augustine. Bare-faced *flouting* of traditional canons and reticences, however, challenges the basic validity of time-encrusted dogmas and traditions, is stigmatized as intolerable arrogance, and casts the malefactor into a bearpit from which he is not likely to emerge "alive".

Unfortunately for highly-sensitive professional clergymen, volunteer work within the administrative structure of church and synagogue, notably during this period of their decline in prestige, does not always attract the most generous-spirited, compassionate, and "civilized" members of the community. Dedicated service in the areas of social reform, political renovation, and enlightened philanthropy compete successfully with "the vineyard of the Lord". Men and women of broad horizons and vision who occupy themselves with any of the multiple "activities" that busily seek human energy in any modern religious institution may retreat in dismay from the petty politicking and personal jealousies from which a religious organization is no more exempt than any other that must rely on unpaid votaries and are therefore tempted to exploit normal human vanity. Under the circumstances, the strong support given to Russell Horsburgh by a considerable segment of his church membership reflects credit on both.

As to Horsburgh's opponents, would it be fair to suggest that the most vehement among them might have been subconsciously hurtled into the maelstrom by a sense of their own guilt? In the complex skein of motivation, psychiatry would assign a prominent place, I think, to the "dirtiness" of the sex-act with which Christians of pristine fundamentalism are often indoctrinated. The "original sin" taint handed down from primal Adam may have more endurance among compulsive churchgoers than our sophisticated era realizes – and it does not grant immunity even to absolute monogamists. . . . Would thoroughgoing psychoanalysis reveal festering remnants of guilt-feeling in the subliminal underground of the more vocal crusaders in the Chatham morality-squad?

The lurking guilt-complex of Christians deeply conditioned by vestigial Puritan fear of sex has been aggravated by the New Testament admonition against sinning with the eye or the mind. (If the eye lusts, "pluck it out".) If visual or cerebral lechery imperils one's state of grace in an environment where mini-mini skirts, nude movies, and lurid books aid and abet the labors of Satan, few of Horsburgh's lay or clerical enemies will approach the pearly gates with equanimity.

I dare to entertain the possibility that the erotic facts and fantasies described so vividly in "Portnoy's Complaint" are in kind if not in detail part of the mental furniture of most normal male (and female?) adults in Christendom, whatever their faith, no-faith or vocation (the pulpit not excluded). The now-familiar post-Freud process of projection and transference *could* offer therapeutic self-purification, all the more when directed at a hired minister who had made himself vulnerable by what may have been only naïve indiscretion. And one's pastor, priest, rabbi is always fair – and popular – game!

The "Horsburgh Affair" has highlighted one of the numerous urgent dilemmas youth is creating for organized religious authority today: the sex-revolution. The cumulative signs of this revolution do not pass unnoted by clergymen who shrink from speculating about the virginity of both male and female youngsters who stand before them to take the vows of marriage. In all likelihood the trend will not be reversed – until our decadent "Western civilization" collapses into its self-created mire and must begin from scratch to rebuild socially-constructive values and institutions, or until nuclear war leaves only a few living survivors to renew the human adventure in a latter-day "Garden of Eden" (which, as a southern United States Senator piously observed, must be inhabited by Americans).

Shall the church and synagogue still further validate the

charge of "irrelevance" by clinging to and peradventure sinking with the old morality – or shall they scuttle it, in a gesture of defeatism and self-disarmament, to remain afloat? The prospect in either case does not invite optimism.

Russell Horsburgh tried to meet the issue head-on by luring nubile youth into the precincts of the church. Who knows? With the understanding and cooperation of genuinely sophisticated and realistic laymen he might have contributed the educational value of a well-intentioned and brave experiment to the problem. Now, through Youth Anonymous, he is attempting to bring the ministrations of a religion-oriented discipline into the confused lives of the young – reversing direction but retaining the aim and purpose.

In the meantime, clergymen inevitably experience in their own persons the corrosive and at times demoralizing impact of radical change in sex standards and the level of acceptability in the realm of private conduct. Statistics on the lessening appeal of the clerical vocation in Protestantism, although not necessarily related to troubled concern with the problems arising from sexual freedom, may be a secondary effect of their cumulative influence. The agonized self-examination of Roman Catholic priests no longer able or willing to be celibate reflects not only the "aggorniamento" and "open window" dream of Pope John XXIII, but also a reaction against the ages-old exaltation of anti-sexuality as a road to salvation. The more naturalistic and life-affirming emphasis in Judaism has blunted the time-bomb impact of the sex-explosion in the personal experience of rabbis – but there are signs that the permissiveness that middle-class Jewry grants to youth has begun to impinge sharply on Jewish spiritual leaders striving to keep alive ancient and tested moral guidelines.

Some denominations (notably, I am told, the Anglican) have conducted surveys on the sexual problems, attitudes, and opinions of their clergy. A number of the questionnaires have been analyzed and their findings published. Such candor and courage recognize a progressively-deepening problem, and hew out a path to grapple with it. Some day such candor and courage will be the rule rather than the exception, and trauma such as Russell Horsburgh's descent from pulpit to prison – and, hopefully, his ascent back – will have shed light along the way.

Rabbi Abraham L. Feinberg

I DO NOT CRITICIZE PERSONS, BUT ONLY A STATE OF AFFAIRS. IT IS THEY, HOWEVER, WHO WILL HAVE TO ANSWER FOR DEFICIENCIES AT THE BAR OF HISTORY.

— LIDDELL-HART

PREFACE

The ancient Greek myth of Sisyphus describes a man who is condemned by the gods to push a stone up a hill. Whenever he reaches the peak, the stone slips and rolls down. The gods thought that there would be no worse punishment than to perform ceaselessly a task that accomplishes nothing. In this story, I find a remarkable companion in Sisyphus. Like him, I have treated certain gods with levity, though my gods differ in name from his. Like him, I find a joy in my humanity and try to provoke a similar joy in others. Sisyphus is punished by the gods Jupiter, Pluto, and Mercury. I am punished by the gods of hypocrisy, narrowness, and scorn. He is destined to toil at his rock until it veritably becomes a part of him. I seem destined to bear my stigma until it too becomes one with me.

Albert Camus, the French philosopher, has written that Sisyphus finds triumph within his punishment. His descent from the top of the hill grants him the time to reflect on himself, to be superior to his rock-fate, and to scorn his tormentors.

I hope that this book becomes my parallel to Sisyphus' triumph. It is my descent from the hilltop of a life's work. Its outline follows roughly the pattern of my life, describing my ideals as a clergyman, my practices within each congregation and, finally, my confrontation with the law and the pent-up opposition to me in the city of Chatham. It is a combination of reflection and personal history. It tells my side of the story. In doing so, it provides my vindication. I expect to find my burden once again at the bottom of the hill; but I also expect to point to my deeds and to find that the struggle itself grants a victory. Camus says that one must imagine Sisyphus happy. I can understand that sentiment.

This book is divided into three parts. The first outlines my convictions and subsequent actions as a minister of the United Church of Canada prior to my call to Chatham. In the second part, I have written about my ministry at Park Street United Church and about the events leading to, during, and after my arrest on charges of contributing to juvenile delinquency. Finally, I have summarized the conclusions drawn from my experiences as a clergyman and the hopes that I still hold for the Church.

I am deeply in the debt of the Rev. R. C. Smeaton for his efforts on my behalf and for his timely, penetrating book, *THE HORSBURGH AFFAIR*. It has provided an excellent answer to the charges against me and has rallied tremendous support for me from its readers.

My especial thanks also go to the Rev. G. Morton Paterson for his assistance in editing this book, and for his unflagging support – in countless ways – during the entire crisis.

My lawyers, Charles L. Dubin of Toronto and C. Emerson Perkins of Chatham, have continuously been courageous and articulate in my defence. Without their patience and insights I could not have continued my fight to regain my good name.

There have been times during the past two years when I have had to rely entirely upon the financial generosity of others. The late J. Wesley Jorden, Chairman of the Committee of Stewards of Park Street United Church, Mr. Roy Leslie, and twelve business associates in Chatham spearheaded "The Legal Aid Funds". I can never hope to repay Mr. J. C. Pierce who carried my bail for the four years. The Board of Evangelism and Social Service of the United Church of Canada has given me a compassionate grant to alleviate my living expenses. The Sudbury Presbytery and the presbyteries of the Saskatchewan and

Manitoba conferences have forwarded generous contributions. Two of my former churches, St. Paul's in Sudbury and Zion in Hamilton, have raised funds for me. In Toronto, Miss Helen R. Craven and the leaders of the "Horsburgh Legal Aid Fund" have canvassed the business community. The willingness of these people to donate such help to me – in some cases, to a complete stranger – has left me with an invaluable sense of aid and comfort.

Space does not allow me to list those whose letters, conversations, and benedictions have sustained me. Such a list ranges from willing reporters who have listened and then carefully documented my story, to the Company of the Damned whose members, scorned for some reason by society, have worked to avoid a similar fate for me. I have received, with gratitude, letters of hope and blessing from people within and without the Church. I am thankful for every one.

Youth Says Cleric Taught Him More Than Can be Repaid

Ac

By DON

Telegra

CHATH
clergyman
ported wh

Woman: Chatham P

By RON LOWMAN
Star staff writer

CHATHAM — A woman member of Park Street United Church said yesterday its minister's morals were of the highest and she had never heard anything like his lecture series on "The Modern Crisis on Sexual Morality."

She thought so much of them she had taped them for the future use of her son.

The woman described Rev.

Favor Susp Charged Cl

TORONTO (CP) — When a clergyman is charged by police with an offence he should be relieved of his work —with salary protected—until the case is settled, says The Observer, offi of the Unit Canada.

"It is under presbytery he this action f

PART 1

THE PHILOSOPHY BEHIND MY MINISTRY

sed Minister Praised

TEVENSON
Reporter

— A young
day he sup-
rtedly what
Rev. Russell Horsburgh tried to achieve in sex education and other matters.

The young man was one of seven character witnesses who appeared in court here this morning in Mr. Horsburgh's trial for allegedly contributing to juvenile delinquency.

Cross-examining the young clergyman witness, Crown Attorney Blake Ward challenged

stor 'Friend, Father

nding
gy

blication
urch of

le that a
to take
it pre-
judices, i
public, th
man cha
torial in t
The twc
to Rev. R

Sudbury Support For Horsburgh

St. Paul's United Church, Regent St., was the scene Sunday night of a Service of Intercession and Appreciation for Rev. Russell D. Horsburgh, of Chatham, recently convicted on five charges of contrib
to juvenile delinquency
given a year's prison ter

A large group of fr
from the Sudbury are
tended the service to te

THERE IS A TRUE CHURCH WHEREVER ONE HAND MEETS ANOTHER HELPFULLY.

— JOHN RUSKIN

CHAPTER 1

I am a clergyman. You wouldn't know it to look at me. I used to look like one. I wore a pulpit gown. My clerical collar showed the world the part I was playing. But gown and collar are gone. And instead I wear garments of disgrace. For, you see, I have been in jail. On a bright, June morning of 1964 I was arrested in my church office in Chatham, Ontario. I was tried by the courts that summer. I was convicted that fall. And all because of a crime I did not commit.

I am not complaining, for I have simply joined the ranks of thousands of men and women who have been put in prison for crimes they did not commit. In fact, I am joining the ranks of many ministers and priests who have been condemned by the very society that they loved and tried to serve. Mine is a long story, a story that is more true to the history of Christianity than are the cozy tales of those revered knights on white chargers who coddle thousands of North American congregations with the promise of a sweet and forgiving Jesus. The history of the church winds from jail cell to jail cell, and I am honored to be in that procession.

The church has always been called to love the world; but always there has been a core within the church that felt that she should love only that part of the world that is lovable! The nice people. The predictably upstanding citizens. The people who don't get drunk. Or get thrown into jail. And when that core is invited to love that part of the world that is unlovable – the tax-collector, the harlot, the publican, the delinquent youth, the addict – a howl rises to the heavens, which is a continuation of that frightful howl at Golgotha: "Crucify him!"

I have been the minister in two kinds of congregations: those in which the "core" relinquished (not always willingly) their favored position, and those in which they fought tooth-and-nail to keep their high seats. I had seen how other ministers have fallen victim to subtle expulsion from a congregation when their pulpit or their practice had bitten too deeply into the hide of community prejudice or injustice or corruption. I had read of churchmen in history who suffered frightfully at the hand of congregations they tried to serve. But never did it occur to me that my own ministry would be put into jeopardy by savagery in one of my congregations. Never did I suspect that the madness of Golgotha would reach into my own life as it had reached into the lives of so many others. Never did I expect to see the day when a modern lynch mob would be whipped into a false accusation, and that the mob would be made up of those I had come to love most – the young. How astounding that my ministry of trying to push back the barriers between church and world, of trying to link Negro and white, couth and uncouth, should consolidate a small group of die-hards into a vigilante squad bent on my destruction.

It is not because my story is unique that I now lay before you the making of a minister. Neither is it because I feel that my story is exemplary or heroic. It is, rather, because mine is the story of so many men in the history of the church that I have a duty to lay it bare. If mine is a tragic story, it is not one of personal degradation but one that shows up the sore on the side of so many churches. I am a typical minister and my association has been with a typical North American denomination. That my name reached headlines is due to the extravagance of my style and its twisted exposure in an Ontario courtroom.

My story begins in a farm-home in the southwestern Ontario

village of Fordwich. I recall an urge from boyhood to someday become a minister. One cannot document reasons for the dreamings of children, but a faithful church-going family was the first seed in my development. Rural congregations are seldom vanguards of social action; but, there must have been something about the congregation and its ministers that fascinated a rather ordinary youngster and made him think of himself as someday serving the church. The church had a fair share of everyday conversation in our home, and I can recall the vigor of church-union discussions in 1925. The United Church of Canada came into being as a big and rather floundering organization, and for some years our village made certain that both Presbyterian and Methodist backgrounds were shared in a year-about use of the buildings and the care with which men were called to the pulpit.

After the usual vocational uncertainties of a young man, a brief encounter with banking, though satisfying, gave way to the compelling urge to apply for acceptance as a candidate for the ministry of the United Church. My work in young peoples' groups gave me the main glimpse into what the church was for, and it seemed to me then that if the church was *for youth*, then I would gladly be a part of it.

At the recommendation of the elders of a local congregation, I was received as a candidate by the Bruce Presbytery in the Hamilton Conference of the United Church of Canada. I enrolled at McMaster University in Hamilton, and, although I was to be officially connected with Westdale United Church as an assistant to the minister, I had opportunity to hear men in various pulpits in the city.

It was the personality and approach of Dr. E. Crossley Hunter, one of the great, even legendary, figures of the United Church, who inspired me with greater zeal for my calling. From his pulpit there blazed a fiery yet compassionate gospel, one that he described as both workable and sensible. Great congregations responded to this gospel for daily life. I can remember imagining how it must be to preach as he did. Sunday after Sunday, as I listened to Dr. Hunter and thrilled to his fresh and vital insights clothed in simple eloquent speech, I indulged myself in the audacious excitement of putting myself in his place. My homiletical training began at his feet. More than he ever knew, he was starting me on my way.

There were many influences upon me in those crucial and formative college years. But in looking back it is clear that the single most impressive mark made on me was the ministry of Detroit's Dr. Merton S. Rice. Religion as an inner experience of God expressing itself outwardly in a passion for social righteousness, this in many ways became the theme of my growing concept of the gospel. He spoke of the demand for a ceaseless labor for the weak, helpless, and downtrodden, and he clothed his message in sound scholarship and magnificent pulpit artistry. But it was the practical side of Dr. Rice's style that moved me most, because he fought unsparingly against the evils of poverty, prejudice, and oppression. In our day we are seeing the church moving out of the sphere of community social action and handing it over to government or other secular agencies. It is difficult for us to feel the exuberance of Dr. Rice's conviction that religion is the supreme centre of social service.

None of the men who entered theological schools in the immediate post-war period fully knew what kind of preaching would be demanded of the church. We were being ordained to serve in a church very different from the one in which we had been raised. New patterns of ministry were going to emerge in communities we would be called to serve, because the war had jostled the church as it had the world. At Emmanuel College in Toronto, theological study was a fascinating excursion into the history and current stance of the church. Here was not a pageant of doleful prelates, but a dramatic meeting with popes, bishops, saints, seers, heretics, and martyrs, each making a contribution to the developing church. Inevitably, some courses emerged as favorites, with theology taking second place to the practical subjects of Homiletics and Christian Education. I remember Dr. A. S. Orton, Professor of Homiletics, who taught the art of preaching. He gave to his students a contagious demonstration of impeccable sermon construction and phrasing, sincere pulpit presence, and masterful technique.

As the years have passed in my busy life, I have found that the theological books in my library have steadily drifted to the top shelves where they lie fairly undisturbed, whereas books on psychology, sociology, literature, history, and politics lie on a level where they can be easily reached and used.

I went to the United Church College in Winnipeg for my final year of theology. Under the tutelage of Dean E. D. G. Freeman I was given a view of the grandeur and completeness of the gospel. His lectures formed the basis for what I was later to call a person-centred, full guidance, understanding of the gospel and the ministry. He urged that the church has a responsibility to persons from birth until death. The church was described as an institution that deals with people across all the seasons of life. It is a place in which a man is understood in his totality, including his sinfulness. The church has its reason for being in helping people move through all life's stages under the power of God within them. Each man must search for a higher level of self-understanding as he grows in tolerance, respect, and love. Life is a maturing, an ever-deepening freedom in relation to God and one's fellows.

I had an opportunity to try out these theoretical ideas of the gospel in summer mission fields in Northern Ontario, Saskatchewan, and Alberta. But the domestic routine of keeping house in my "house of a thousand drafts" and the sheer roadwork involved in serving three to five congregations made it impossible to fully work out these principles. While I was on mission fields I was able to engage in vacation schools and camping; but, for the most part, farmers scratching out a living on poor land did not really sense that the church was for them.

After ordination by the Hamilton Conference in 1947, I was settled on the Creighton Mine charge in the Sudbury Presbytery. During the two years that I was there I tried to fulfill my philosophy of the gospel in my ministry. My main interest then, and always in my later ministry, was a youth program. At

Creighton my ministry began with the starting of a lively youth group, and the pattern that was to mark my approach to young people for twenty years took shape. It was a program dealing with varied interests and problems, not doing everything for the young people, but preparing the activities in such a way as to encourage active participation. A youth group was started at Lockerby, another point on the charge, and it too was built on this general plan. I have always found that a successful ministry to youth will result in the subsequent attendance and participation of parents, not only in the youth program but in the overall church activity. I tried to remember the names of each adult, youth, and child in the church and to avoid neglecting any member. A close contact with the parish keeps a minister aware of the needs of individuals and families. The church program must range over all age and interest groups; but I have found that sound youth work is the central focus of a church's action.

A lesson I learned in working with youth is that here is a place where individual personality shines out most clearly. At no other point is the importance of a person-centred ministry more obvious. In the churches I have served, such a philosophy has been tried, and the result has always been a growing membership and greater attendance at worship and mid-week meetings. Again and again I have admonished those who worked with me to keep an eye on individuals, realizing that nothing matters in the long run except what happens to them. What happens to the church as a whole will follow naturally. A truly Christian church must be personality-centred, and its criterion of value, or success, the saving experience that comes to individuals.

If this be true, then the minister's relationship to the members of his congregation must not be based on a handshake at the church door. There must be more than an occasional interest in groups and a street-conversation about politics or the weather. What a pity when a minister withdraws from his parish, preoccupied with other things such as administrative duties, and instinctively shields himself from first-hand knowledge of his people. It is not uncommon to see a minister, called to intense contact with people, hide from any more than a superficial meeting with his people.

Yes, at Creighton, and in churches afterward, I learned that a minister must dare to leave his study, to go into the streets and into the homes, to learn what people are really like, what they really do, and what they really need. Even though he must have the help of laymen who are ready to share and take responsibility in the developing of these creative relationships, he himself must not avoid direct participation with people. And yet, how often have I been reminded by others that ministers are expected to be isolated and aloof from life's raw facts, ignorant of its smut and dirt, its sordid sin and passionate debaucheries! No minister ought to live in a world apart or to remain in an ivory tower. He must be willing to share in the struggle of human souls against every kind of guilt until he can imagine no revelation of evil that would shock him. He must do so, and yet be able to stand outside the experience sufficiently to be able to help the sufferer reach out of his guilt.

With such a philosophy, a ministry directed to individuals in their need, I tried to act in the situations confronting me in the early days of my work. Only in this way did my work in counselling have any point. Only in such a way would my words from the pulpit strike home and hit nails on the head. It was not at Creighton but on my next charge that I was to discover that this kind of ministry has risks as well as rewards. Relevance to life can get close to home and can threaten the most precious citadels of one's personality. I was soon to discover that a minister must be involved in a very real tension if his work is to have a cutting edge. But the gospel is the first example of the risk of being involved with persons, and I interrupt my story to point out some of the danger points and highlights of the ministry of Jesus of Nazareth.

CHAPTER 2

Religion begins with the doctrine of man – his potential, his heritage, and his destiny. It is not a lowly destiny – but a high one, and the Psalmist says it best: "Thou hast made him a little lower than the angels, and crowned him with glory and honour". Jesus did not declare divinity for himself when he ministered in Palestine; rather he declared the divinity of all human beings. He saw in every man a potential to rise to a divine height. The great personalities of history stand in this tradition – of disclosing the greatness of the human spirit. The religion that I would preach is that which can disclose and heighten a man's potential.

True religion is to love God; but God can only be reached by man's loving man. By love I do not mean maudlin affection, but rather an attitude of unbreakable goodwill toward every man, no matter who he is or what he may have done. I mean an attitude of encouragement toward him that will draw out the best that is in him. This is well portrayed in the New Testament kind of love, because Jesus is constantly standing in front of people who are depraved, misshapen or socially outcast. In each of these situations, He speaks or acts in such a way as to bring out some hidden potential. For this He was often criticized by those who claimed to represent "right religion," and to some it even appeared that because He loved the untouchables of His day He must Himself be an untouchable. ("He is possessed by

Beelzebul, and by the prince of demons he casts out the demons.")

Paul gives his famous definition of love in the thirteenth chapter of First Corinthians; but in the Gospels themselves there is only an "acted" definition. It appears to contain at least these ingredients: the *will* to see good in the most outwardly depraved individual; the *capacity* to think good about every human being; the *ability* to feel the thoughts and feelings of another; and the *power* to act out the will, capacity, and ability that have been mentioned. Starr Daily, who was once an incorrigible criminal and a "lifer," and who was converted in a prison dungeon, gives the best definition of Christian love that I have ever found: "Real love does not complain or blame, or justify a negative view about a person. It sees its own reality in everybody. It obligates no man, exacts nothing, commands nothing. It cannot give according to calculation. It is automatically self-giving, taking no thought of any reward or returns for service rendered. In the absence of real love, religion is without God – a form, a shell, an empty husk. There is no real discipleship when real love is not present. 'By this shall all men know that ye are my disciples, if ye have love for one another.' By real love we are born again. We then do the works of real love and bear its fruits. We no longer argue about religious doctrines, or defend ourselves and our way of life. Love needs no defence, academic discussion, proof. By its fruits we know it. Under every provocation it remains kind, creative, redemptive, victorious, and absolutely fearless."

If this was the kind of love expressed in the life of Jesus, then can anything less be expected of the church, which is pledged to embody His life in our day? Religion is loving God through loving man; and the church is under a divine directive to reach out in love to all men including those whose lives are torn and mangled by personal and social sin. The first duty of the church may be to praise God; but this is only meaningful in the underlying action of compassion for the poor and social concern for the outcast. The great prophets announced such a social gospel and were usually stoned for it. But despite the reaction from the community the church has no choice but to meet the needs of the outcast (the twentieth-century leper) – the alcoholic, the addicted, the juvenile offender, the emotionally disturbed. Sadly, these people are so often just the ones overlooked by the church and such a church is nothing more than a social club – "The Society of Those Pleased with Themselves". Such a group has insulated itself against the very ills in society that it was called into being to meet head-on.

This is the broad kind of hope that I had for the congregations that I would serve, and I did not doubt that the kind of love demanded could indeed be lived by a church. Every minister begins with starry-eyed optimism, and fully expects to see glimpses of the Kingdom itself in his first few appointments. Most of my work in early pastorates was immensely satisfying to me and, I believe, to the Boards with which I worked. But it was not long before I could sense that the church was capable of veering away from its mission, and that it could become a most pernicious institution. After having served the Creighton Mine charge for two years, I was called to minister to the newly formed congregation of St. Paul's in Sudbury. The church had been meeting in a house, and in my ministry there we met in the basement section of what was to be the church building. A program was developed that met the social needs of many groups in the congregation, and boys' work and youth work were high on the list of activities that buzzed around the building. We erected a gymnasium to meet the recreational needs of people. The congregation attended faithfully not only the regular morning service but the series of evening programs on somewhat controversial issues. During one winter the church held a series of twelve evening talks on "Understanding between Roman Catholics and Protestants". An attempt was made to reach the youth, for whom the words of the popular songs of the day were as well known or better known than the words of the Gospels themselves. One way to bridge the gap between the hit-parade and the gospel was to preach on the songs themselves, and sermon titles were these: "It's in the Book", "I Believe", "Too Old to Cut the Mustard". Fireside programs were held after the service, with talent provided by members of the congregation.

Everything was going fine; two things happened in St. Paul's, however, which were to recur again and again in my ministry. The first was the emergence of an "old guard" (even in a new congregation!), and the second was the quiet but deadly beginning of gossip. Although neither problem reached very dangerous proportions at St. Paul's, I ought to have been forewarned that they could happen in a dimension to ruin my ministry only twelve years later. The old guard was a small group of people who had had a considerable share in the original planning and erection of the building. From the fact that the physical home of the church had been their responsibility they derived the unrelated conclusion that they ought to be the custodians of whatever happened *within* the building from that time forth. It is quite likely that they did not realize themselves that this assumption underlay their whole attitude to me and to the other people who would be part of the congregation. When it became clear to them that they would not be permitted to have what amounted to a veto on church programming, five families in this group abruptly left the church. This was an unhappy way for their selfishness to be eradicated from the congregation; how much better if they had been willing to put their shoulders beside those of the others and work out a compromise life together. But I had seen how stubborn church officials could be and how remote from their motives was the simple principle of love.

No continuing crisis developed from this departure of old power; but before I left St. Paul's gossip began to surround an unknowing young bachelor minister. A married woman was engaged to handle some of the secretarial duties of a growing congregation – and her office was placed in the vestry. When it reached my ears that stories were circulating about this proximity of our working areas, we agreed that it would be best if she did her office work in her home. I gave her permission to take the church typewriter to her home; but to my astonishment it was not long before two members of the Board of Stewards went to her and insisted that the typewriter must not be off the church premises. It was removed at once, and "confusion" is the only word to describe the way I felt about the whole episode; and confusion plus some behind-the-hand chatter gave birth to gossip that was to follow me to other churches that I would be serving. As the gossip circulated from family to family two groups were soon disclosed: one that believed implicitly in the totally unfounded stories, and one that refused to give them any credit. No open battle ensued, and certainly there were no suggestions at any Board meetings that I was being made the subject of some juicy tidbits. My only reaction was to ignore the gossip, for I felt then that to "fight" it would only serve to fan the already smouldering talk. Of course, gossip begets gossip, and it was not long before my great interest in boys' work became the earth from which more stories sprouted. By this time I was involved in boys' camping at Fairbanks Lake Camp, the United Church summer camp just west of Sudbury. In addition a Tuxis and Trail Ranger program at the church and Saturday morning basketball meant that a good proportion of my time was spent in the company of teen-age boys. Usually a church is delighted when the minister takes an interest in youth work, and I felt that there could be no better way to exercise my ministry to youth than to be with the boys in their many activities. But the gossip about the church secretary joined arms with my obvious interest in young boys, and a double-barrelled whispering swept through the church corridors. Not only was I accused of an affair with the church secretary; I was branded a homosexual as well!

I must underline the fact that at the time neither the old-guard jumpiness nor the false gossip gave me any great cause for concern. Any person in the public eye comes under the scrutiny of so many types of personality, and it would be ruinous for him to take too seriously the ruminations of cranks.

Since the explosion in the church in Chatham, I have talked to other ministers about the problem of shallow gossip, and so many record the sadness and even terror of knowing that people to whom you are trying to minister are spreading foul slander. Phone calls, anonymous letters, but worse still the quiet murmurings after meetings – these are only some of the ways in which men of the cloth, as well as other public figures, are victimized.

I mention the situation at St. Paul's to show that within the church, which is called to love, there can be the basest kind of "unlove". Yes, a church is a body of human beings, and as such it is capable of the same jealousy and envy that eats into the heart of any organization. University faculties, business corporations, even camp staffs – all these are prime targets of the "green-eyed monster". That it strikes the church as well is perhaps not too surprising; but it raises the question that too few dare to face: In what sense, then, is the church a *redemptive* fellowship set in the midst of an unredeemed world? If the church is in turmoil because of internal squabbling then there is no energy left for reaching out in service to needy humanity. Strength is wasted in trying to simply maintain the family, and the wretched, the poor, the afflicted are bypassed and ignored.

Another facet of church "politics" became clear while I was in the Sudbury area. (It will be shown later in the book that this was a part of the unsavory background of the Chatham episode.) One of the very disturbing things about the Christian ministry occurs when young ministers leave the protective shelter of the seminary to go out into the parish ministry, that is to find that redemptive love is notably absent amongst clergymen. Often when a young minister becomes seemingly popular and successful he is resented by his brethren in the ministry. Jealousy, suspicion, and distrust quickly become obvious forces working at meetings of ministers in the area. The impression that a greenhorn minister receives is that all will be well in ministerial relationships if everyone settles for a low-grade mediocrity. One ought to be a pawn – a yes man – with no individuality or ambition or dreams that might set him apart from the others. Sometimes I have thought that one can only survive in this profession by serving up pap and tranquilizers to a congregation. Let a man dare to step out of line and out of the pattern of black-gowned conformity, even in this enlightened generation, and he runs the risk of being branded as maladjusted and in need of the psychiatrist's couch.

One of the disillusionments of our day – made more pointed by Pierre Berton and those like him – is the fact that the *typical* pattern of congregational activity tends toward the negative one that I have just indicated. It is shocking that a comparison with the New Testament ideal of church life reveals almost the absolute opposite to church life as most of us know it! Furthermore, hatred and envy in the church are no mere unfortunate pocks in an otherwise unblemished body. They are sins against Christ himself, and make of the church an "anti-church". Paul had high hopes for the church: "For ye are all children of God by faith in Jesus Christ. For as many of you as have been baptized into Christ have put on Christ. There is neither Jew nor Greek, there is neither bond nor free, there is neither male nor female, for ye are all one in Christ Jesus." Surely this means at least that Christians must be able to sacrifice even of their personal demands in favor of the needs of the body to which they belong: the Body of Christ, i.e., the church. Hence, any offence committed against a fellow-member of the body is an offence against Christ himself. This fellowship is to be no jovial social club; it is to be notable for its acts of love. The twenty-fifth chapter of Matthew shows this unmistakable quality of the church as illustrated by Jesus: "When I was hungry, ye fed me. When I was thirsty, ye gave me drink. When I was naked, ye clothed me. Inasmuch as ye did it unto one of the least of these my brethren, ye did it unto me." But the church's practice is so often at variance with its teaching. Disturbing, restless questions arise in the mind of so many members of this body: How can I believe in the mystical body of Christ when some congregations in our day refuse to accept a colored person into its fellowship?

How can the church be so oblivious to the needs of people in its immediate area – the poor, the anti-social, the underprivileged? How can the church, if it is really imbued with the real presence of Christ, be such a hive of suspicion, intrigue, and enmity?

But I am ahead of my story, for it is not at all fair to say that my pessimism regarding the church's life reached these proportions while I was at St. Paul's in Sudbury. There occurred the first flutterings of what was to eventually become a total disillusionment; but my ministry at St. Paul's from 1949 to 1953 was a period of growth and enrichment. I was beginning to feel confident that my approach to youth was sound and that my pulpit ministry was such as to hook into the lives of people in the pews with force and relevance.

When the call came from Zion United Church in Hamilton I was thrilled. For here was a church bordering one of the areas of Hamilton that a sociologist might call "low-income, approaching slum". It was my implicit understanding of the call that those qualities of my ministry that had developed during my time in Sudbury were regarded by the Board as suitable for Zion Church. Our first joint endeavor was to completely renovate the sanctuary, to replace the dark panelling, which created a funereal atmosphere, with something more expressive of joy. The congregation consisted of people who lived in higher-income areas of the city and who travelled some distance to church, as well as those living on modest means in the immediate area. The combination was a happy one. There was no evidence of strain between economic groups. Doctors and lawyers sat on the same boards as shopkeepers and laborers. The stage seemed set for a fruitful ministry and, until 1958, I lived through a period of great personal satisfaction.

The negative forces of "old-guard"ism or malicious gossip were not too evident at Zion. There were indeed members of some Boards and on the Sunday School staff who took great pride in accomplishments of the past, and they would frequently delight in reminding their associates of the way things used to be. There were times when they showed an unbending resistance against new ideas or new persons on the Boards; but on the whole their influence was not destructive. Some of the gossip trailed me from Sudbury, and I was given reason to believe that some of the stories were passed to my new congregation at Conference times and at other gatherings of delegates from across the Province. This did not receive a wide hearing among the members of the Zion congregation; it was not until I went to First United Church, Waterloo, after five happy years in Hamilton, that the gossip picked up new steam.

As I had hoped, the youth program at Zion was an energetic one and lay members rose up to share the leadership in boys' work as well as in teen-age clubs. The meetings of the Young Peoples' Union covered a wide list of topics, and I recall very few meetings in which the room was not filled. The young people decorated a "youth centre" downstairs in the church, equipped it with a television set and a library, and at stated hours during the week they were free to drop in for a chat with someone or watch television. (At this time, early in the 1950s, very few homes in the area had sets of their own.) The two gymnasiums in the church received constant use, and in every respect the building was being put to its intended purpose. It was really a place of fellowship for young people of all ages.

During this time there were many opportunities to speak on behalf of boys from the area who found themselves in trouble with the law. Time after time I went to the courts and stood with a bewildered parent as a judge gave a sentence to a youthful and often tearful offender. I did not shy away from people who were "toughs," and when the young people decided to institute a "Teen Town Dance" on Friday evenings I fully realized that there would be nights when trouble would develop. We made it an absolute rule that neither smoking nor drinking would be permitted; but inevitably there were those who were able to smuggle in a bottle of cheap liquor. I was recently reminded of an incident that took place during one of the Teen Town dances. A scuffle had developed on the dance floor and I was quick to investigate and try to stop it. Some boys with liquor on their breath were swinging at one another, and I was struck in the eye and knocked down. There was a near-riot for a few moments as the word got around the hall that the minister was flat on his back on the floor! But when I was on my feet again and the fight was dispersed, the dance returned to normal. We always had a number of adult counsellors on hand to assist with any trouble-makers we would have to handle. There were frequent expulsions from the dance; but never did we tell a person that he would not be welcome at the church. We made it clear that his being put off the premises was because of his destructive behavior.

Dancing has always seemed to me to be a very creative and healthy form of social expression. The young people were very diligent in the preparations they made, and on special occasions during the year they sponsored dances with a theme – St. Patrick's Day, New Year's, and others. There was no rowdiness at these, and how satisfying it was to meet parents at some of the dances who had come to enjoy themselves with their teen-agers. Every New Year's Eve we held a family night party, with dancing, games, and just "fun". A watchnight service at midnight welcomed in the new year. These were occasions of family fellowship, and it was remarkable that the young people looked forward to this time of having a good time *with parents.* In a time when the distance between many teen-agers and their parents is over-emphasized, it was gratifying to see one group in which this distance, whether real or imaginary, broke down.

Such a program of recreational and social outreach to a community is often condemned for being "too worldly". But why should not a church be a centre for every conceivable kind of helpfulness to a community? Churches that do otherwise, or that at any rate avoid contact with the human needs of people, seem to me to deny the very reason for their existence. I am familiar with a situation in a city in which I lived where two churches of the same denomination are only two blocks apart and face what they choose to call the depressed area of the city.

It is from this area that the largest number of youths is hailed into court. Yet these two churches do nothing to touch those youths. They do not try to help them, and when challenged, they make the excuse that such work belongs not to the church but to community agencies. What a travesty! Is it any wonder that people are saying with increasing gusto that the church is irrelevant. If those two churches were to close, it is sad to remark that they would not be missed by the very community in which they stand. In the twentieth century we have seen the greatest burst of concern for the socially unacceptable that the world has ever experienced; yet, many churches relate to such people with nineteenth-century tongue-clucking.

Few in the church realize the extent to which city youth almost literally make their home in the streets because there is no other place that will have them. They tire of the novelties of fads and yearn for a place where they can feel that there is something bigger than a fashion or a "kick" to sustain them. Some take to coffee houses and find something enduring in the guitar-singing fellowship. It is possible for the church to provide such facilities for youth; but most congregations regard young people as nuisances and allow only the best behaved to invade the sanctity of a church building. By their attitude they are conditioning a new generation to hate the civilization into which they were born. I would even say, without fear of contradiction, that many churches follow policies with regard to youth that *promote* rather than *hinder* the growth of rebellious delinquency.

Later in my ministry I was to hear this kind of church policy expressed in a nut-shell by a public-school principal, the father of two children. "Only decent young people should be allowed on church premises . . . all others should be kept out!" This kind of statement is contemptible coming from a so-called churchman. For one thing, I do not believe that it is necessarily true that young people from successful homes are negatively influenced by those who have trouble at home or with the law. My experience has been just the reverse: those who come from stable and loving homes are able to extend a mighty influence toward those who are less fortunate. It is cruel selfishness to teach a child that he must always associate with children who are his "equals" or his "betters". The Christian child should be led to see that he can be like leaven, that his influence can be for good in situations that are bad. On the other hand, he should also be taught that he can learn something good even from people who give a first impression of being good-for-nothings. A child who welcomes relationships with people different from himself stands a better chance of having a good life than the one who is taught to withdraw from unpleasant personalities.

Again, Jesus is our model. He was all-inclusive in His friendships. He did not bar anyone from being among His associates. He was called the friend of publicans and sinners. The Christian, if he is to live on this model, is to give to people with whom he stands, and he is to give without regard to the "worthiness" of the receiver. This is surely the sane Christian social philosophy for the child of a Christian home. He will be warned that this kind of life will often mean disappointment and that he will even be exploited on occasion for his open-handed love. But he will be more of a man or a woman than if he had snivelled behind the skirts of a matronly philosophy of "being with the right people at all times".

Two things can be said here about an interest in young people, particularly those branded as "problem children". One has to do with the child. The other has to do with those who try to help him. Karl Menninger, the noted psychiatrist, published a penetrating book called *Love Against Hate*. In the first chapter, "The Medicine of Love," he contends that real love is the best therapy in the world for personality sickness. A multitude of psychological failures in adults can be traced back to a time in the emotional development of childhood when he was deprived of love, or just as seriously, when he thought he was being deprived of love. Certainly the most important need of every child is to be loved, to be believed in, to be appreciated. Without that his sense of security is threatened, his belief in himself is undermined, and he is made to stumble. Jesus speaks of the regard he had for those who prevented children from reaching their best – reaching the Kingdom: "it is better that a millstone be hung around their neck". To steal love from a child is worse than stealing his vitamins or his daily glass of milk: he could live with poor health, but he could not live with a warped spirit. He would be dead even though his body functioned and he appeared to be alive. How frequently I have made the definite plea to parents and to those who lead young people: never, never let any child think that you do not think much of him, that you compare him unfavorably with others. Every child in the world can do something well, and it is for adults and parents to help him find the maximum expression of his personality.

Most youngsters that receive time and energy from an adult leader respond with enthusiasm, and in their later life they often point to lessons in life that they heard or experienced at an organized church youth group or in Boy Scouts or Guides. In recent months I have had occasion to return to Hamilton from time to time, and have chatted with young men in their mid-twenties – some engaged in doctoral work at university, some fledgling businessmen – and to reminisce about good times – and hectic times – spent at Tuxis or Trail Rangers some ten years ago.

But for every young person who responds to leadership there is another who does not. Every group contains those who have been so robbed of a feeling of significance that they do almost anything to disrupt a group; yet, they must remain part of the group. In many ways it is the "problem youngsters" in a group who provide it with zest and interest for an adult leader, because here is the challenge in its most pointed form. But it also is the place where a leader's nerves are most sorely tried, because he never knows what kind of behavior will result from ordinary situations.

The case of Donald in the documentary film "The Quiet One" is repeated in the lives of many adult youth leaders.

Donald has been drawn from his slum environment and placed in a treatment centre for disturbed children. Withdrawn and moody, he is suspicious of his counsellor, Martin. Finally, after patient work, Martin breaks through to Donald, and the young lad seems to accept his counsellor on a relaxed and friendly basis.

Soon afterwards Donald sees his new friend laughing and talking with another boy. The shattering thing is that the new boy is lighting the counsellor's cigarette with his lighter – just as the counsellor had let Donald do! This was a privilege that he had thought was his alone. He is shaken. The counsellor is not all for him alone after all. Donald can no longer be really certain of his real acceptance. In despair he runs away. But before he goes he steals the counsellor's lighter from his pocket.

Donald's flight from the treatment centre and his act of thievery are not really hostile acts, except to the person who has no inner eye. They reveal a desperate need for love. Donald could not get enough of his counsellor's attention and interest. And at the point where that love was beginning to make an impression the little fellow could not share it. The theft was to symbolize – in a way that his words could not have done – how much he wanted Martin, or something that was Martin's.

This kind of lesson and its need for acute discernment was learned by many adult church leaders with whom I have worked. It is disheartening that people who step forward to volunteer in a youth program are sometimes sneered at by those who have "more important" church functions to perform. I have been encouraged and upheld so often by adults who assisted me in a ministry to youth, and for the most part they have always remained loyal in the face of carping criticism. It is difficult to work with youth – so exasperating – but also so gratifying. Laymen who have worked with me have realized that one must be willing and ready to suffer the most unexpected kinds of rebuffs from young people, and often just at the time when it seemed that progress was being made. Leaders must be prepared to submit to a kind of social crucifixion at the hands of those who do not understand the redemptive process of love and who in anger turn a vengeful hand seeking some irrational judgment on a leader. Judas' betrayal may have been a covert act of love to his Master, more so than the cowardliness of Peter or the confused flight of the other disciples. I have encouraged lay-leaders to realize that young people too, if disturbed at a crucial moment in their life, will act out their hostility in anti-social behavior on those who are trying to do most for them. We have heard the expression, "they bite the hand that feeds them". But this hostile act is very likely an attempt to "speak" to a person in the peculiar language of action. They may intend that the results of their behavior will be a great show of love or an even deeper kind of acceptance. Such behavior can be a kind of test of the sincerity and limits of the newly developing friendship.

From a ministry at Zion Church where my understanding of youth work became secured in a broad program of outreach, I was called to First United Church, Waterloo. Again, it seemed to me that one of the terms of the call – and the most important – was my emphasis on youth programming, and I accepted. During five years of daily contact with young lives my sensitivities had been sharpened and Waterloo was an opportunity to use the tools that had been so prepared. But during my two years there, another aspect of life became clearer to me: the working of the *adult* mind. If my years at Zion revealed the nature of young people to me, my brief residence in Waterloo was to bring into painful focus the nature of the typical adult mind in the church.

CHAPTER 3

Negative forces can be inspired by the adult leaders of a congregation among their fellow parishioners; these forces began to appear at Waterloo. Allow me, however, to suggest first some positive possibilities. Although my main work has always been in the area of youth, it has been absolutely essential that this be backed and supported by adults and parents. Without question, the main requirement for a sound youth program is a sound and harmonious adult-minister relationship.

What kind of relationship should this be? First, there must be a climate of mutual acceptance and basic trust. Naturally, the church is not the only place where these qualities are important, as any organization, large or small, suffers if they are missing. But, with the church, it is a heightened requirement, because everything suffers a slow and sickly death if the congregation feels that there is serious pull between the minister and some (or all) of the Board members. It is particularly difficult in our day for the minister and his people to be of the same mind, for our age of rapid transition demands that the minister be a nonconformist. To be worth his salt he may indeed have to be a radical, calling for the partial or even total change of some aspect of church or community life. Only by so doing can he effectively make religion relevant to changing times. But the attitude of a congregation to their minister is vital at this point.

It can break him or make him, render him useless or help him scale heights of insight and service. The hearer has a profound effect on the speaker and not to hear is to make the speaker mum. Jesus was unable to perform any "mighty works" in some towns because of their failure to hear what He was saying to them. A congregation's health depends upon the minister's courageous speaking and the peoples' faithful response.

Hence, the minister must be many things in a congregation – all of them tied to a basic courage. He must be a leader, teacher, celebrant of life, minister of the balm of experience and concern, inspiration and sympathy to the harrassed and confused. He is also irritant and gadfly, a *provocateur* of great causes or, in the words of the ecclesiastical saw, comforter of the afflicted and afflictor of the comfortable.

The adult layman is not a passive "follower" though; he must share in the active outreach of the church. He is a contributor to the life of the whole Body, of the whole church, a participant in worship and study, and, most of all, a participant in the loving outreach and service to the community and to the fellowship itself. If his church affiliation is one of integrity he will do everything within his power to see that the church's family unity is maintained and strengthened, and by so doing he will help to add to his own balance in life. He will be a valued and valuable person in himself because he is working for the essential value of all the people with whom he worships and plans. He has a duty to think, speak, and act from the motive of "building up the Body of Christ".

How does this work out in practice? Naturally, there are many times when there is an underlying harmony that binds together minister and layman into an effective force for power and good. There were such times at Waterloo. But how quickly did feathers ruffle when a pulpit word was too far off the track of conformity, and how rapidly did some Board members begin to suspect that my usefulness to them would be impaired by a too radical departure from things-as-they-were. It is well to remind congregations that they do not *hire* a minister to preach as they bid, in the sense that those who pay the piper also call the tune. This is a common understanding of the relationship between the minister and the congregation. If this happens, they insist that the minister spare their vices and flatter their follies, that he prophesy smooth things: a merchant of mush and purveyor of pablum. Such a congregation will restrain the minister from doing and saying what they know full well he should do and say. And by shackling their minister they shackle themselves. Any minister who consents to this ignoble concordat should have written over his pulpit EMPTINESS AND DECEIT.

One particular pulpit series drew forth a storm of protest, not least from the Session of the church, i.e., the Board of Elders. The series was entitled "The Christian Understanding of Sex, Love, and Marriage". Speakers were invited from many professions to share their insights with the predominantly young congregation – many from the University. Mrs. J. D. Taylor, President of the Canadian Council on Education, Dr. John Frid, a medical doctor from Hamilton, Dr. Wilfred Boothroyd, a psychiatrist in a Toronto hospital, and Dr. J. Hoskins, General Secretary for the Y.M.C.A., were among those who preached from my pulpit. The reaction from young people was one of heartfelt appreciation. But the reaction of many adults was that this topic should not grace a Christian sanctuary. Some of the Elders insisted that the word "sex" be stricken from the advertising, and rumors began to circulate that the minister had an abnormal interest in sex. Although the main planning for the series was done by a group of students from the University, it nevertheless seemed obvious to many that I was treading on thin ice by encouraging such discussion of life in the church!

This series and the "abnormal interest of the minister" that it illustrated, was enough to fan into life the Sudbury gossip to which I have referred earlier. From the beginning of my ministry at Waterloo there was one person who seemed bent on my destruction, and who very early began to spread innuendo about my past. He was prominent on the church boards and an altogether respected and trusted member of the community. Surely any stories that he passed on must have truth in them! So when he began to circulate the odious nonsense that I had an affair in Sudbury, and that without doubt I was known for homosexual behavior, it received a willing and ready audience. I was to discover later that his accusations would not be restricted to the time that I was to remain in Waterloo, but that he was going to become a self-styled inquisitor, making certain that the city of Chatham and the Presbytery of Kent were fully informed about the perverse clergyman now in their ranks.

I was being gradually awakened to the raw fact of hate within the Christian fellowship, and it was only to become clearer during my Chatham ministry. Anyone who has experienced the sheer inertia of much church work can surely point in the direction of lovelessness and rivalry within the fellowship as the root cause. One is reminded of the too-frequent question of people to whom the Christian foreign mission is extended – and of the following anecdote. An African matron once asked the local lady missionary, "We cannot make out why you came out here to tell us how to solve our problems, when you can't even solve your own!" "What do you mean?" asked the missionary, shocked and indignant. Had she not made a tremendous sacrifice, left home, learned a new language, put up with inconvenience, sacrificed a good income, and all for the sake of the gospel? "Well," said the African matron sullenly, "you three missionary women can't get on together in the mission house without quarrelling, for all your Christian upbringing. How do you expect us to believe your religion will help Africans to live together?" The missionary spent most of the night in tears of shame. She felt she had denied her Lord. For all her talk about love, she had never learned how to love.

Let there be no mistake about the fact of "unlove" within the typical Christian church today. Grudges remain long after the event, jealousies erupt and drain energy from boards, Sunday School staffs, choirs, and even team ministries. Someone has said that for a real fight you cannot beat either a family quarrel or a church squabble! What a shocking testimony to the wholly empty cup that we offer to the love-hungry peoples of the world – a gospel of love in which there is no love. We hold up only the possibility of love as shown in Jesus; but it remains possibility only and not reality. And yet, to say all this sounds like a thoughtless and sweeping charge of hypocrisy – and it sounds superior. So let me hasten to add, with shame, that this same unlove is often basic to my own ineffectiveness.

Having begun my ministry in Creighton in 1947 with every hope for a fruitful and full life, I was now to enter a phase that would tumble to the ground my bright idealism and faith in the church. In 1960 I was called to the pulpit of Park Street Church, Chatham, and in the baggage that went with me there was a vast assortment of articles. They ranged from a gentle optimism toward youth work – a feeling that disappointments would be only minor exceptions from an otherwise successful ministry – to a sturdy caution toward fellow adults who would be sharing the responsibilities of programming. The accumulated experience of thirteen years in the Christian ministry went with me headlong into the crisis that was to terminate my association with the church denominational.

Dances Called 'Game of

"I'll turn tragedy to t

Went to Accused's Church
For 'Sex, Morality' Series

Cl
Pr
By

'Horsburgh Inst

Horsburgh case co

PART 2
OPERATION CHATHAM

g' | Counsel Blames Teen-age Clique For Trouble

mph" says Horsburgh

's Youth ams Praised tnesses | Found Guilty On Five Charges

ment Of Devil?'

d reach legislature

TO BE LIBERAL IN SOME COMMUNITIES MEANS TO BE SENT TO PRISON, OR EVEN THE GALLOWS; WHEREAS IN OTHER COMMUNITIES IT MEANS BEING LOOKED UP TO AS WISE, WELL-BALANCED, AND CIVILIZED.

— PROFESSOR CLARENCE SKINNER in *Liberalism Faces the Future*

CHAPTER 4

Park Street United Church. An old, dull-red, and somehow stately building, it stands in chill dignity at the intersection of Dufferin and Park streets in Chatham, thrusting tall towers at the benevolent sky. I well remember the day I arrived. It was the first Sunday in the New Year. As I walked eagerly along the street I felt that here, the largest United Church in southwestern Ontario, awaited a challenge that would be the greatest test of my ministry. Here would be an opportunity for service that, I felt sure, would put an unparalleled gloss on my career.

Alas, I was quickly disillusioned. From the first, I found a familiar, stagnant church situation. There was a morning service on Sundays, a Church School, a few sporadic meetings, and little else – the shell of Christianity, Christianity encrusted with tedium and half-heartedness. Park Street Church consisted of a building, a preacher, and parishioners who came to him only on Sundays. By-products were a few social gatherings, some organized societies with no apparent purpose, and a flickering interest in missions. In short, this great church to which I had come with such fervor and excitement of purpose was little more than a self-contained club, socially beneficial to its members, perhaps, but possessing an idea of Christian outreach that was limited to a frowning, critical attitude on moral questions and to desultory get-togethers that started without purpose and ended without objective. A shallow witness was what I found, one that simply did not reach out to all sorts and conditions of men.

I discussed this disheartening situation with the Pastoral Relations' Committee and later with the Church Board. There were a few ripples of concern, a spark of ambition. We agreed that we didn't want to be a self-contained club ministering to ourselves alone, but that we would try to express our Christianity in service to the community at large as well.

Obviously, in a city the size of Chatham, only a wide, all-embracing program would meet the mosaic of need: loneliness, unemployment, a lack of recreational and character-developing activities for the young, and a lack of uplifting, nourishing pursuits for the mature. Not just a Sunday program, but a seven-day-a-week program – vigorous, wide-spanning, dynamic!

And why not? We had the facilities. Our building was ideal. And only by reaching out into the city and the world with a broad spectrum of Christian service for all, could we fulfill the tremendous potential of these times. Hard work? Of course, and welcome. I fell to the task with pleasure and enthusiasm.

We did not, however, impose a program on the community. Rather, we asked the people what they wanted and drew our blue-print accordingly. One part after another of our program came into being, not because we planned it but because the community created it. And it wasn't long before our church bustled with activity throughout the week, so much so that sometimes our problem was not how to get people to come but how to involve the crowds when they arrived. It was, of course, a question of priorities.

A social service department was a "must" from the start. Employment is seasonal in Chatham, with many families on welfare half the year. So a clothing and food distribution centre was set up, later to become one of the finest projects of my twenty-year ministry. Scores of families and individuals were helped under the plan. Clothes and food flowed in and out of the church in a heartening, continuous stream as the people happily responded to this tangible means of making Christianity relevant and meaningful at last.

The youth program alone bristled with possibilities. Traditional activities for parish children were indeed present on a small scale; but there was no attempt at all to reach young people outside the church. Result? The Young People's Union and Tuxis Boys' Club were started. Then a "Teen Town," soon to draw more than 500 teen-agers every Friday night, was organized. Eventually, the gymnatorium and basement hall were packed with happy youngsters playing, and, in their own way, learning the wholesome teachings of religion and brotherhood of men until they were too tired to fight, steal or molest.

Then, slowly, these young people began to join the congregation and to attach themselves to and take an interest in some of its groups and activities. Indeed, within three years no fewer than 600 had allied themselves with fifteen church organizations, and at Easter, 1964, (ironically, a few months before my ministry ended) another hundred joined the church – one of the largest surges of membership in the congregation's history!

Meanwhile, the youngsters were organizing volleyball, badminton, ping-pong, billiards, and shuffleboard, and soon six church basketball teams were competing in city leagues. Eventually, "Teen Town" was changed to include some of the glamor of a teen-agers' night club in a bid to attract young people who were frequenting undesirable places and getting into bad company. In this connection, we realized that, if a healthy atmosphere could be provided in the church on Friday evenings, teen-agers would find no attraction in other, more questionable places. Tables were arranged around the gymnatorium, decorations were put up, lights dimmed, floor shows planned, bands brought in. Sometimes – and this surely was a sign of the community's support of the enterprise – local business firms sponsored the evening program, paying the bills, putting up prizes.

Before long, the church was open seven days and nights a week, even on Sunday afternoons. For youth, the church increasingly became the centre of their thought and, inevitably, a useful influence on their lives.

Youth Anonymous was another project that had its roots in the "Teen Town". One night five boys swaggered in, half drunk. As we believed in welcoming every youth who came to us, the student minister on our staff tried to handle the situation in a manner that might eventually win these boys for the church. With firmness and kindness he persuaded them to leave the dance but urged them to return the next day to take part in recreational activities. They did so; then, – a triumph of understanding – asked if there was a church club they could join. This was the start of Youth Anonymous in Chatham. At this time, the student minister wanted to do something about the growing number of boys causing trouble at the dances; so, he sought to organize them under the auspices of the church. With the approval of the Christian Education Committee, the experiment was begun.

In those days, only two other Youth Anonymous groups were active in Canada – at All People's United Church, Sault Ste. Marie, and at Eastwood Baptist Church, Hamilton. Youth Anonymous has a national reputation in the United States, where it was founded in 1954 by Professor Albert Eglash of the Psychology Department of the University of Michigan, and Ernest Rumsby, an ex-convict re-established by Alcoholics Anonymous. Backed by the Detroit Rotary Club, Mr. Rumsby and his supporters turned Youth Anonymous into one of the most remarkable agencies combatting juvenile delinquency. Members may have clashed with the law, be on probation, have a suspended sentence or be on parole – the only qualification for membership is a determination to correct twisted thinking and to lead a better life. The Youth Anonymous open meeting is the key to the movement's success. Members meet in group therapy sessions to share problems and experiences and, guided by adult counsellors, seek ways to work with society instead of against it.

Youth Anonymous, in essence, is a spiritual program founded on the unlimited love of God. As in Alcoholics Anonymous, which it reflects and is patterned on, there is a serenity prayer: "God grant me the serenity to accept the things I cannot change, courage to change the things I can, and wisdom to know the difference." Its steps form guideposts for every meeting and are the principles by which Youth Anonymous operates.

THE 12 STEPS

1. We agreed at times we couldn't control ourselves and our lives had become unmanageable.
2. Came to believe that a Power greater than ourselves could help restore us to proper thinking.
3. Made a decision to turn our will and problems over to the care of God as we understand Him.
4. Made a searching and fearless inventory of ourselves.
5. Admitted to ourselves, to God and to another human being the exact nature of our wrongs.
6. Were entirely ready to have God help us remove the wrong things in our character.
7. In our own way ask Him to remove our defects of character.
8. Become willing to make amends to all we have harmed.
9. Make amends to such persons whenever possible.
10. Continued to make our own inventory and when we were wrong promptly admitted it.
11. Sought through prayer to gain a better understanding of God and ourselves, praying only for knowledge of His will for us and the strength to carry that out.
12. Having learned from these steps we passed this knowledge on to others.

Within a few months our Youth Anonymous group had grown to seventy members. Then a girl's group was started, the two sections coming together occasionally in co-operative projects. I have had training in social work, spent a year at the University Settlement House in Toronto, and worked for college summers in community recreation in slum areas of Hamilton; yet, I say unhesitatingly that Youth Anonymous is the most effective antidote to delinquency that I have yet found. In my Chatham memory, the most moving testimonies of personal transformation and new directions found originated in this group, bearing real witness to religious reality. These young people may know little about religion and less about theology; but, what they do know is that in their helplessness they were introduced to a Power greater than themselves, through Whom they found a strength that now made possible a victory that had seemed beyond their ability. I have listened to many learned arguments about God; but, for honest-to-goodness evidence of God, His power appropriated and His reality assured, give me a meeting of Youth Anonymous every time!

Another innovation – our Sunday evening program replacing the usual service – provoked wide comment. Discussions, forums, films, drama, collegiate nights, musicales, lectures followed each other over the year. Ours was the first Protestant Church in Canada to open its pulpit to a Roman Catholic priest. From that same pulpit the congregation heard two rabbis, an astronomer, a renowned Canadian poet, the Prime Minister, a reformed convict, a negro preacher active in the civil rights movement, a professor of philosophy – all specialists in their fields, and all relating their experiences and learning to workable religion. And, even more significant, all of them brought to our people the pristine truth that God is for all men. Yet, tragically, it was on this wide, multi-tapestried altar of worship that our bright new structure of service and Christian outreach later foundered, a structure brought down by prejudice, resistance to change, and, incredible though it seems to the logical mind, the sheer perversity of a handful of misguided souls who couldn't bear to see something bold and hitherto untried succeed.

CHAPTER 5

The perpetual conflict in the Chatham congregation had been brought to my notice long before I took up the charge there. Indeed, one Chatham man, familiar with my radical ideas and methods, had warned: "You'll meet your Waterloo if you go to that conservative church." Its turbulent 125-year history had long been the subject of comment in clerical circles.

One fire-brand minister was banned, I knew, because his outspokenness upset the congregation. Another was asked to leave because the congregation tired of his repeated references to war. Another was victimized by a false story of his having had an affair with his secretary. Just the same, it was apparent that most of the parishioners were heartily sick of the mud-slinging and desperately wanted to get along with the new minister. On the fringes, new people waited to join the church as soon as the gossip and friction subsided. So, walking a tight-rope, I got along. The slightest change raised eyebrows, of course; but no one was in a mood to take issue with the new minister and, cautiously, I tried to keep it that way.

It is impossible, however, to keep a tiger leashed for long. The chasm between the old way and the new approach demanded by this vibrant, modern age could not be bridged. It wasn't long before meetings of the Session (Elders) and Official Board degenerated into outbursts over the simplest change that broke with the past.

I had always believed that a minister new to a church is expected to make changes. He must hope that the people will patiently and courteously study the new ideas and, if they are acceptable, embrace them with enthusiasm. This had been my experience in past churches and no rebellion had resulted before. At Chatham, however, although we were drawing more members and reaching out to the community in a vigorous way, a fractious few were determined to scuttle every radical program I suggested. "The church should move backwards before it moves forward" was how one elder put it. Most criticism was levelled at Youth Anonymous. Although the program had been upheld by the Christian Education Committee and approved by both the Session and Official Board, the traditionalists dismissed it as a symptom of modernism. They said it lacked the dignity required of a church group. They denounced it because colored youngsters could join.

Youth Anonymous embarked on two projects a year that would benefit the community. One was a concert by Marion Anderson, the world-renowned contralto. When the promotion started, a long-time elder told the press: "People around here aren't going to pay five bucks to hear a colored wench sing." And his wife snapped: "They'll lose their shirts!" In fact, Miss Anderson drew a capacity crowd and held it entranced for two hours. Later, the die-hard group sought to undermine a concert by Virgil Fox, the organ virtuoso: but he, too, triumphed.

Clothing and food distribution, also, came in for criticism. The old guard carped that welfare was a matter for city hall and, when that attack was turned aside, they then demanded that all clothing be packed for the poor overseas rather than for the poor at home. Inevitably, the enterprise died – a victory for prejudice and shallow thinking.

Another sizzling issue was that of Negroes joining the church. They were accepted in youth groups, and it did not occur to me that they would be barred from the congregation itself. To me, racial discrimination in any church is unthinkable. When two Negroes attended their first service at Park

Street, however, they were greeted with outright hostility. People already in the pew moved out. Later, when they formally joined the church, I read out their names to the gathering, but made no mention of skin color, and at the reception service the Negroes came forward with others to take their vows.

Then the storm broke. One elder resigned because, he said, I preached too much about racial matters – "almost every Sunday" were his words. (In fact, when I checked my sermon file I found that I had referred to race only twice in eight weeks, and then only briefly and superficially.) A woman elder demanded: "Niggers have their own churches – why don't they go there?" A heated argument followed about interracial marriages as though the only purpose of Negroes joining the church was to find a white mate. Later, two more Negroes joined; but they were treated with such coolness and distaste that they soon withdrew. As far as I know, that church standing so proud and yet so sadly aloof at the corner of Park and Dufferin streets in Chatham is still segregated, and we are all the losers for it.

By this time, the church program was burgeoning on its own. It had been hammered out in the Christian Education Committee and Session, and approved by the Church Officials. Indeed, we had already agreed that it was not my program but a child of the community. Despite these measures of approval, my opponents were now trying to force me out of the church. Most of the members stood beside me and I owed it to them not to leave when patience and persistence might yet win. When I offered to resign, the Board refused to listen; so, I continued to hope that the conflict would resolve itself. It never did.

About this time I received a letter from one of the elders, copies of which were also sent to all members of the Session:

After considerable thought and with deep regret I have decided to write to you regarding conditions at Park Street United Church. Such conditions are far from satisfactory. In voicing this opinion I am bespeaking the views of many others besides myself.

The things to which I take exception can be classified under three headings – youth activities, the Sunday evening lecture series, and pastoral duties.

First – in regard to youth activities.

I have no objection to a social time for young people on a Friday evening. I also have no objection to a restricted amount of social dancing always provided there are added features on the programme. What I do object to, however, is set out below –

(a) Dufferin Hall on Friday nights has become nothing more nor less than a public dance hall. Anyone of suitable age who has the price of admission and shows evidence of sobriety is apparently qualified to attend. As a consequence every type of individual is present. To my mind it is unfair to the young people of our own church to have this condition prevail. If the social evening (including a limited amount of social dancing) were for our own young people and their friends, a balanced programme of recreation together with something more constructive could be worked out.

(b) Under today's conditions, and I am not condoning them, it is unfair to have a mixture of colored and white young people brought into close recreational contact. These young people are at a romantic age and there is considerable danger involved. I am sure most members of the church would agree and feel badly if any of their own young people should marry someone of a different color. The children of such marriages are likely to have a difficult time in life and there is no use inviting trouble.

(c) Youth Anonymous is undoubtedly a worthy project but which should be carried on by one or more social workers as a community project. Giving these potential delinquents the use of our church facilities and a proportion of our minister's time is unfair to our own membership whose use of the church may be interfered with and to those members who wish to receive the benefit of more pastoral visitation. The sooner Youth Anonymous is out of Park Street Church the better. We have a large group of our own young people which continues to be our main responsibility. Any youth programme should be centred around them.

Second – in regard to the Sunday evening lecture series.

Many of these lectures were good and appropriate to the occasion. These speakers brought a religious message which was helpful to those in attendance. However, this has not always been the case.

Having a Jewish Rabbi occupy the pulpit during Lent, [My note – The Rabbi spoke on Brotherhood Sunday and brought an appropriate message], *giving a Roman Catholic Priest the opportunity of espousing his viewpoint on religion and filling up the programme with non-religious lectures is handing the people a stone when they are crying out for the Living Bread. Chatham is, I feel, spiritually comotose and badly needs the religious flame rekindled in the heart of many a church member. I was astounded and left the auditorium in disgust and silent protest when you followed up a fine Sunday evening evangelical message by the doctor from the Sick Children's Hospital with a series of secular songs right in the church auditorium. An altar call would have been more appropriate.*

Third – in regard to pastoral duties.

I believe there is a tremendous pastoral job to be done in our church and which should be the principal concern of both ministers. The average non-attending church member may not be such a spectacular problem as 18 or 20 outside delinquents but they are more of a primary responsibility just the same. Both ministers should be spending a reasonable proportion of time visiting these people regularly and systematically, discussing with them their spiritual condition and bringing them back into the fold if at all possible. How much visiting is being done apart from calls on the sick and infirm? If I were a minister and saw an average of 500 to 700 adults out of a resident membership of 1732 in church on a Sunday morning I'd be seriously concerned. Perhaps you are but there is only one way to remedy the situation and that's by action. People do have an interest in vital religion if it is properly presented and it's the pastoral obligation to make them realize the transforming influence which an acceptance of Christ can have on their lives. Too many are drawing on the spiritual heritage of our forefathers but salvation is a personal matter and demands an individual choice from each of us individually.

When I submitted my resignation from the Session some months ago no one except . . . (Chairman of the Nominating Committee) asked me why I had done so. The criticism set forth in this letter covers at least some of the reasons for my regretted decision. It was only a small part, if at all, that I resigned because of other commitments. I felt at the time, and still feel that I would like if at all possible to avoid acrimonious controversy but unfortunately things have progressed to the point where I feel compelled to register the points set forth in this letter.

I have an impression that your heart is in youth work more than it is in regular pastoral duties. Under such circumstances both the church and yourself would be happier and render more effective service if you were able to arrange an early transfer to activities of this type.

A few days later I received another blistering letter from this same man:

My letter to the Session was mild in comparison with my true feelings in regard to the way Park Street Church is run under your dictatorship. You have a smooth and brainwashing approach which beguiles an audience, but if you think of it you must realize that your neglect of the large membership of the church in favour of outsiders is a disservice to the very cause which you are committed to espouse. If through indifference nominal church members are neglected in favour of outsiders the case of the kingdom suffers in the final analysis. . . . Needless to say, you won't be bothered in future by seeing my face in the congregation when you are preaching. We have absolutely no intention of transferring our membership from the congregation but propose attending only when you are absent.

This man did not give up easily. A few weeks later he sent Board members a copy of this story, which appeared in the *Toronto Daily Star*:

NON-CONFORMIST PASTOR HAS CHURCH POOL TABLE

In the gymnasium of Chatham's staid Park Street United Church stands a colorful monument to the pastoral individualism of Rev. R. D. Horsburgh – a pool table.

Its history?

"I was disturbed by reports," says Mr. Horsburgh, "that some of our underage young people were frequenting local pool halls illegally. I decided to remedy the situation. Hence, the pool table in the church."

The reaction?

"Among the young people enthusiasm. Among a few others – well, let's say the walls practically fell in!"

However, Mr. Horsburgh is not one to be fazed by ecclesiastical earth tremors. He has induced many in his day.

In a series of sermons on "Love, Courtship and Marriage" which packed his evening services, Mr. Horsburgh said, "I would rather that my son marry a colored girl than marry a Roman Catholic. The racial problems would be easier to solve than the religious because they're only skin deep!"

In Chatham, where a third of the 30,000 population is Negro, Mr. Horsburgh was widely criticized for his remark.

"The color problem is not limited to the southern United States," says Mr. Horsburgh. "There is a color bar in Chatham. Park Street Church, 120 years old and with 2,200 members, hasn't a single Negro on the roll."

Since becoming pastor of Park Street two and a half years ago Mr. Horsburgh has made many innovations.

He launched an enormously popular Sunday evening lecture series – "Adventures in Understanding."

A year ago he founded "Youth Anonymous," a group which, in Mr. Horsburgh's words, "is set up to assist problem thinkers among youth."

"The success has been tremendous," says Mr. Horsburgh, "Today's young people will grasp a helping hand if only the church will extend one. From 4 to 6 p.m. every day I devote myself to counselling troubled teenagers and there is always a line-up outside my office."

During Mr. Horsburgh's pastorate, attendance at evening services has climbed dramatically.

"I try to be sensational," he allows. "After all, if anything in this world is sensational shouldn't it be vital Christianity?"

A deputation from the Board went to talk to this man; but, he refused to see them. Several returned the clipping to him without comment; but one wrote him as follows:

Thank you for sending me the clipping with respect to the Rev. R. D. Horsburgh's work at Park Street Church. This article, I believe, is an excellent tribute to the work he is doing in the community. We at Park Street are undoubtedly fortunate to have a minister so devoted to the problems of our day and at the same time willing to stand for his convictions in striving to do something about them.

A look at this complaining man's background showed that shortly before I came to Chatham he had left St. Andrew's Church over a dispute with the minister and officials over the placing of a decoration in the chapel. In spite of what he said in his letter, he did transfer from Park Street Church and now attends another church several miles away. Every Sunday he drives past the two churches where he was once a disgruntled member, and past a third United Church, to attend his newly adopted church home.

What an opportunity for leadership this complainant missed! At no time did he try, with me or any other member of our staff, to change the conditions he found so disturbing. Nor did he even express dissatisfaction with the program. He simply resigned from the Board, giving pressure of business as his reason. If only he had been willing to talk things out, or had revealed his true reasons for resigning, what a different story might have been written! For all I know, he might have been used mightily to bring harmony to a divided church. He resorted, instead, to the tactics of the coward and drove the wedge deeper, creating a greater rift than before.

When I was minister at Zion United Church, Hamilton, I

instituted a somewhat similar program and once again a few reactionaries in the congregation opposed the innovations. But there, an old medical doctor, one of the saintliest men I ever knew, who had been active in Zion for over fifty years, a member of the various boards and teacher of the adult Bible class, assumed another role. He was venerated by the congregation as counsellor and friend. Even the reactionaries found him approachable and would take their complaints to him freely. He would listen patiently, encourage no controversy, then make his reply: "He is our minister, isn't he? Then, we must support him." This man was the best friend any minister could have. There were almost fifty years between us in age; but this did not preclude understanding. We abode always in a unity of mind and heart, and this bond never frayed. If any tension was evident in the congregation, it invariably yielded to the patience, gentleness, and goodwill that made him the man he is. Today, in his nineties, he has just retired from his medical career and until recently was active in his various capacities in the church. He was named Hamilton's Citizen-of-the-Year not long ago. If only every church had at least one of his calibre!

During our four years at Park Street Church, many letters in praise and support of our program reached my desk, letters such as this:

Dear Mr. Horsburgh:

Our sincere best wishes for your continued work at Park Street Church and especially with the young people of Chatham. In this modern age it is indeed gratifying to know that we have in our midst someone who is unafraid to stand for what he believes to be the truth. Rest assured there are many young people who are better for your guidance.

May your future be as bright and promising as it deserves to be. Chatham should be proud of the gentleman you have shown yourself to be. More power to you . . . we're with you.

Yours sincerely,

And the more I read and heard, "More power to you . . . we're with you" the more I felt I had to carry on.

CHAPTER 6

Despite the persistent assaults on our efforts to make religion relevant, no evidence existed of any exodus from the church, although many people still wouldn't come because of the treatment meted out to previous ministers. The old guard continued to boycott my services; but they always managed to be re-elected to the various boards, mainly through the connivance of a nominating committee whose structure hadn't changed appreciably for several years. I tried to break this unfair pattern.

At the Easter Communion, two months before the axe fell on me, we welcomed 123 new members into the congregation – more than had been received in any year of the church's history. This sparked the fury of my opponents. By every devious means, they tried to prove that new members were obtained by questionable methods. It was unthinkable, they maintained, that under my ministry so many would join the church from worthy motives. One elder took it upon himself to call on some new members, asking such questions as, "Were you bribed into joining the church?" "Did you receive proper instruction from the minister?" "Why would you join a church with the kind of program Mr. Horsburgh has?"

Finally, I received a visit from a parishioner of long standing who said that he didn't feel at home in the church any longer. "So many strangers are joining the church," he complained. "I look around to find my friends and I see all these people I don't know. Might as well be in a strange church." He left shortly afterwards. That man didn't want a church; he wanted a private club. He wouldn't invite these strangers into his home so why should he invite them into the church? And this, in essence, is the heart of the turmoil that raged in Park Street Church.

In the spring of 1964, a few months before my ministry ended, the Committee of Stewards, who had always backed me, suggested to the Official Board a salary increase – $300 for me, and $100 for my assistant. My opponents were outraged and, as a result, they tried to amend the motion to read in favor of the assistant only. Fortunately, the majority of the Board saw the patent unfairness of this manoeuvre and my raise was passed, too.

Living near the church was a member of the old guard who seemed perturbed about the many teen-agers thronging to the youth meetings. By phone calls to me, the church office secretary, and the chairman of the Stewards, he made known his dislike of these gatherings and threatened to call police. Late one night, he and his wife appeared in a lane behind the church and accosted the janitor's daughter as she was saying good night to a friend at the church door leading to the apartment where she lived. "Indecent exposure!" the woman cried, pointing at the girl. When the man asked what she was doing at the church, she replied that she lived there, and opened the door to call her parents. The couple promptly left, but the girl and her mother decided to follow the matter through and went to the trouble-maker's home, demanding an explanation. The man pretended ignorance of the incident but his wife spoiled it for him by saying that they had seen the girl with no clothes on. The fact was that the girl was wearing tan shorts and white blouse and was, of course, fully clad. Had her mother not taken the matter up with the couple immediately, an ugly smear might have gone around the community and the girl's reputation might have been jeopardized.

During the weeks following this incident, the usual complaints from these same two meddlers streamed in, until, finally, the Chairman of the Stewards investigated the rumors and, finding them without foundation, prevailed on the couple to stop making trouble. They left the church shortly afterwards; but, significantly, they told the church secretary that charges were being prepared against me.

This was not the first sign of a conspiracy mounting against me. In fact, some people in the church were boasting that they were on the inside of a plot. One of these was an elder who had long opposed me and who told a church meeting that I would soon be legally implicated in a morals situation. "But I'm not supposed to talk about it yet," he added. Meanwhile, the couple who had criticized the Marion Anderson concert had started driving around the city urging people to sign affidavits against me. These, they said, were to be given to the Chatham police. Then, one day, a detective phoned my assistant pastor and asked if he knew that I was trying to have him removed from the church staff – the very thought of which never entered my head. (My assistant later reported this strange behavior to my lawyer.) In another telling incident, one woman was heard saying, "We'll get him yet!" She claimed that I had been investigated during my Hamilton ministry and found to be a communist. Indeed, she carried on an active campaign to circulate this gossip.

My supporters in the congregation were by now disgusted with the continual bickering and gossip. They had previously taken little part in discussions at Board meetings; but now they were becoming aroused and sought to end the controversy. They started making themselves heard in meetings, with the result that the old guard was being put on the defensive for the first time. Their threats continued, of course; but I felt that now victory – a happy, integrated, and therefore, effective ministry was at last in sight. I was mistaken. A few weeks later, I was embroiled in a crisis that wasn't to end until my career was in a shambles.

A woman in the congregation appeared as the master-mind of a plot to ruin me. Known for backing projects that caught her fancy, she would assume charge to the point of domination. Then, after several personality clashes, she would bow out of the picture. At a Youth Anonymous meeting, she described herself as a writer looking for a story and volunteered to become the group's publicity director. In due course she joined the church and became active in its work. She went overboard in a bid for the exclusive friendship of the minister. Friends began to warn me that I was heading for trouble if I did not curb the relationship. I was told also that I was not paying her the attention that she wanted and that this could spell danger. One day when I spoke to her about her daughter's misbehavior at the church, she accused me of neglecting her daughter at the Teen Town. I reminded her that all parents had been invited to supervise these youth activities; but, she took offence at this and from that time on she began to work against me.

About this time, a new boy joined Youth Anonymous and began to assume some leadership of the group. His popularity was resented by some of the founding members, however, who felt that he was a "favorite" with the counsellors and with me. This may or may not have been true. At any rate, the woman seized on the situation to align these malcontents behind her, and before long was inviting them to her home and generally turning them against me. She buttonholed some members of the old guard for their support, and finally prepared what she called her "dossier," alleging that teen-agers at the church were engaging in sexual activity with my approval. She delivered one copy of this document to the Chatham police. Other copies were given to some of her other conspirators. She claims that she sent a copy to a Toronto newspaper.

This development was bad enough; but then I got into trouble for defending young people in court, although I do not recall once speaking audibly in the courtroom. My work was done mainly behind the scenes or through lawyers. In an address that I gave to a Chatham service club, I said that putting people in prison was not always sensible. Part of my speech contained the following quotation: "Reform schools should be abolished and replaced by homes and farms directed by trained personnel who had a genuine interest in the welfare of boys, and who did not think primarily of monetary rewards for their work. The system of punishment for boys today is based on a wrong principle – suspicion rather than belief. There is no healing of a wounded spirit in a jail cell, nor redemption of youth in a lash. Our present institutions are doing little or nothing to reform boys. Rather, they are feeding them on the poison of revenge and the red lore of criminality. Reform schools are misnamed. They are really prisons for boys; they turn out youths resolved to take vengeance on society."

My remarks were reported in the newspapers and criticism from some quarters was sparked. I received a rash of anonymous phone calls and letters threatening reprisals. I was told that I was interfering with the processes of justice and that I would eventually get what was coming to me. The Crown Attorney's attitude showed in the disdain with which he treated me when I went to court on behalf of a troubled youth and in his refusal often even to bid me the time of day.

In the autumn of 1963, discipline at the local jail was investigated by a Reforms' Department inspector and, in that I was a frequent visitor there, I was asked to comment. I had no complaints and I gave a favorable report. Nevertheless, probably because of my general comments on methods of penology, it was rumored that I had instigated the investigation: once again I came under fire for meddling.

Then, the beginning of the end. I learned that my work at Park Street Church was receiving the attention of the police. It just seemed natural that this should follow the attacks I had already suffered. Night after night we saw Detective Tom Bird sitting in his car, watching the church from a parking lot across the street. Later, some teen-agers told me that he had questioned them about their morals. I was astounded then to learn that reports were circulating of young people leaving the dances and sneaking into out-of-bounds parts of the building for sexual intercourse. My chaperones were just as shocked. Worse, rumor had it that I was encouraging this traffic.

I immediately phoned the detective and requested to see him. He was shocked that I knew that he had questioned the young people. He finally promised that he would come to see me. Then I phoned my lawyer, C. E. Perkins, who advised me to ignore it. "It's just the continuing attack of the old guard," he said, "It'll soon die out."

But the detective did not come to see me even though he had promised to do so. His investigation lasted for about a month; yet, not one of the large group of adults working with me in the program was questioned – neither counsellors, leaders, chaperones, janitors, secretary, assistant minister, nor anyone else who could have cast the brightest light on the issue. The police spotlight merely scanned the group quickly, resulting not in a fair, balanced appraisal of the situation – but instead picking out innocent incidents that could later be brought into shocking, sinister, and invariably warped focus. As a result, even those young people incriminated by their friends' statements were never given a chance to have their say or the courtesy at least to defend themselves. It was this spotty handling of crucial events leading to my final agony that characterized the whole infamy.

On Monday, June 29, 1964, I was arrested and charged with contributing to juvenile delinquency. It was a day I will never forget. The sky, I recall, was somewhat overcast, in tune with the sombre thoughts that had plagued me for weeks and that, in some way, I knew would not clear until the final confrontation with my accusers. That confrontation was expected, but nevertheless sudden and shocking. . . . Two detectives, Peardon and Bird, walked into the church vestry at ten o'clock in the morning and just stood there, flushed of face and terribly awkward.

"I have been expecting a visit from you for some weeks now . . ." I started.

Peardon broke in, "Mr. Horsburgh, we have a warrant for your arrest." He stood beside the desk, solemn and nervous. He seemed unsure of himself, as though he'd never said these words before.

I fell into my chair. "*What?*"

He repeated his words, then read something from a document. But I hardly heard what he was saying; the shock and disbelief of it all was just now beginning to make itself felt. They were arresting me . . . it was real.

"I'll call my lawyer," I said finally.

"Oh no, you don't need to do that. That can be done from the court," Peardon said abruptly.

I then went to the house next door to change my clothes. The detectives went with me, watching closely as if they were afraid that I might escape their custody. We then went out into the street to the waiting police car and drove a half block to the court.

"I'll never understand why you didn't keep your promise to come and talk this thing out with me," I remarked to Bird. (He had done the investigation.) But all he said then was, "Anything you say now can be used against you in court."

I was taken into the public courtroom and seated in the prisoner's dock. When Magistrate Ivan Craig came to the bench and looked at me, his face turned ashen. Immediately, the prosecutor, who had already been going over the charges with Bird, began to announce the charge against me; but the magistrate stopped him.

"This should be done in the family and juvenile court," he said.

We all left to go there; but, Magistrate Craig suddenly begged off the case and was later replaced by Judge William Fox of London. The charges were read that day; I denied them all. Then they put me on personal bail and let me go home. Reporters and church officials began to telephone incessantly. The story was all over town.

The arrest, the trials, and the conviction that followed were as inexplicable as any part of the whole charade. In all these bewildering happenings, only the church itself remained constant, its twin towers reaching for the sky in symbolic, comforting assurance of the unchanging Kingdom of God desperately seeking fruition and meaning in a world still ruled by man's malice, pride, and stupidity.

CHAPTER 7

Public reaction to my arrest was, to say the least, confusing. The application of Christian principles came from the most unlikely sources. In some churches, I was subjected to more hellfire and brimstone sermons than the devil himself. On the other hand, I won support and friendship from churches I knew little about – Jews, Unitarians, Quakers, Christian Reformed (Dutch) Church, Pentecostals, who were quick to align themselves behind me. I was branded an agent of the devil. I was called a communist and a nazi, a fiend in human form; but I was also hailed as a hero and a true pioneer. Some wanted me lynched; but, there was also a man who changed his will to make me one of his heirs! Some clergymen labelled me a deviate and sought to brand me insane. Yet some clergymen were busy in their churches raising money to help pay my legal expenses.

Between being praised and persecuted, condoned and condemned, I might understandably have become bewildered, particularly at the brand of ethics sometimes displayed by the staunch exponents of Christianity. But of one thing I was sure – and this more than anything else has sustained me – I was innocent of the charges. My conscience was clear. I had no skeletons in the closet of my life. In the sight of God I stood unabashed. This knowledge saved me from depression and anxiety during these long months of fighting and waiting. It brought a peace and a strength that the world cannot give nor take away. I became determined to leave no stone unturned to clear my name.

My own church's reaction was confusing. My supporters rallied immediately to see what they could do to help me. Yet some of those who had most loudly proclaimed their Christian convictions were now most vocal in damning me. I was, nevertheless, moved by the tangible evidence of kindness and generosity that came from every side.

My Church Officials asked me to call the Board together to discuss the matter, in my absence. Another minister was asked to chair the meeting. My opponents, needless to say, turned out in full strength. Those who hadn't gone to church in years and who had, long ago, withdrawn their financial support, were there for the kill.

After much argument, my Officials decided to pay my legal costs, a decision that lifted my spirits immeasurably. There were many things they could have done to side-step criticism. They might have cast me out, remained silent or merely produced a round of platitudes to pacify conscience.

The crucial question was: "Should I carry on my ministry?" My friends wanted me to stay in the pulpit – not only because I was innocent until proven otherwise, but because they felt I should not yield to the old guard whom they suspected to be the culprits behind my troubles. One of Chatham's leading citizens told my lawyer that a local detective disclosed to him that the only evidence they had against me was gossip and hearsay – "but we'll get him out of Chatham anyway," the detective added!

After much thought, I came to peace on the matter of carrying on my ministry. I decided to remain in my pulpit. More people came to my services than ever before. The congregations were made up not of sensation-seekers from outside but of my own people supporting me in a crisis. My opponents, of course, did not come. Instead, they gathered in the same parking lot from which Detective Bird had watched the church and kept a watchful eye to see who did come to church. They never entered the sanctuary. One Sunday, ironically, when our service was broadcast, I announced that a Board meeting was to be held after the service; to our surprise many members of the old guard who were not at the service showed up for the meeting! Obviously, they had condescended to listen to the broadcast!

The crisis did nothing to dampen the ardor of my preaching. Indeed, I felt strongly that God had given me a special message for this hour. While carefully avoiding any reference to my troubles, I found that my experiences just naturally affected my preaching. I spoke on such themes as, "Facing the Future Unafraid", "Keeping Up the Fight", "Faith Born Out of a Struggle," and "How To Handle Tragedy". In all my years of preaching, I never felt more buoyed up by the power of the Holy Spirit and the sympathetic understanding of the congregation. I would not have missed this experience for any price. An inner strength and peace possessed me then that is still with me today.

As I look back now I am convinced that by remaining in my pulpit during those trying days, both minister and congregation gained immeasurably.

CHAPTER 8

It was seven weeks after my arrest before Kent Prebytery made an approach to me. Some ministers who had already found fault with my liberal ministry now demanded that I be removed from my pulpit. Some said I should be defrocked. Following a meeting of their Executive, I was handed the following notice:

After due consideration, it is our judgement that you refrain from all ministerial activity until such time as your case has been completely settled.
We, therefore, request that you refrain from this day forth from all ministerial activity until such time as your case has been completely settled before the civil court.

My supporters in the congregation were a little incensed over the coldness and formality of the approach. They felt there should have been some offer of sympathy, prayer, and help. After lengthy deliberation, representatives of the congregation drew up the following petition:

TO KENT PRESBYTERY OF THE UNITED CHURCH OF CANADA –

Whereas we, the undersigned, are members in good standing of Park Street United Church, A Pastoral Charge within the said Presbytery.

And whereas we have reason to believe that the said Pastoral Charge is in an unsatisfactory condition because of the action of the Executive of the said Presbytery as communicated to our minister, Rev. Russell D. Horsburgh, in a letter from the secretary of the said Presbytery on August 26th, 1964, wherein our said minister was requested to cease to perform all ministerial duties until the conclusion of his trial before the courts of justice.

And whereas the action of the Executive of Kent Presbytery was taken in the absence of, and without reference to, the Officials of the said pastoral charge or of the said minister.

And whereas such action is likely to do damage to the said pastoral charge and the said minister.

And whereas the undersigned believe that the said action of the Executive of Kent Presbytery was taken without knowledge of the accusation made against our said minister or the defences which he has to each and every one of the said accusations and was taken precipitously.

And whereas the said Executive have taken the said action without regard to the admonition of St. Paul in the Fourteenth Chapter of Romans, which reads as follows:

1. Him that is weak in the faith receive ye, but not to doubtful disputations.
2. For one believeth that he may eat all things: another who is weak eateth herbs.
3. Let not him that eateth despise him that eateth not; and let not him that eateth not judge him that eateth: for God hath received him.
4. Who art thou that judgest another man's servant, to his own master he standeth or falleth. Yea, he shall be holden up: for God is able to make him stand.
5. One man esteemeth one day above another, another esteemeth every day alike. Let every man be fully persuaded in his own mind.
6. He that regardeth the day, regardeth it unto the Lord; and he that regardeth not the day, to the Lord he doth not regard it. He that eateth, eateth to the Lord, for he giveth God thanks; and

he that eateth not, to the Lord he eateth not, and giveth God thanks.
7. For none of us liveth to himself and no man dieth to himself.
8. For whether we live, we live unto the Lord; and whether we die, we die unto the Lord; whether we live, therefore, or die, we are the Lord's.
9. For to this end Christ both died and rose, and revived, that he might be Lord both of the dead and the living.
10. But why dost thou judge thy brother? or why dost thou set at naught thy brother? for we shall all stand before the judgment seat of Christ.
11. For it is written, as I live, saith the Lord, every knee shall bow before me, and every tongue shall confess to God.
12. So then every one of us shall give an account to God.
13. Let us not, therefore, judge any man any more: but judge this rather, that no man put a stumbling block or an occasion to fall in his brother's way.

Now therefore, your petitioners request that you, the Executive of Kent Presbytery of the United Church of Canada, withdraw forthwith the said request made in the letter of August 26th, 1964, and support your brother as becometh you in the hour of tribulation.

And we would further request forthwith a meeting with you to bring before you this matter for your consideration as is our right pursuant to section 117 (9) of the manual of the United Church of Canada.

And your petitioners will ever pray.

After this expression of support by a large segment of my congregation, I sent my reply to the Presbytery:

Dear Sirs:
I have given very careful consideration to your letter dated August 26, 1964, and its report of the motion passed by the Executive of Kent Presbytery. I recommend for your perusal Section 165 of the manual which states that "in the exercise of

discipline there should be no inter-meddling with matters that are purely civil."
At the moment, no charges have been laid against me either by my congregation or by Presbytery, and the matter is one of import to the civil courts only.
In the light of the maxim which the church has never once negated; namely, that a man is innocent until proven otherwise, I feel that your judgmental motion and the attitude it implies is of such a nature that compliance with it would be interpreted as an admission of guilt on my part, and would greatly jeopardize my case before the courts.
Consequently, I am convinced and convicted that I cannot comply with your request, but neither am I discounting the right of the church to exercise due discipline when and where deserved. I firmly believe that it is God's will that I continue my ministry as usual in the weeks ahead, as is my right, privilege and responsibility – exercising that ministry which is yours and mine – not because of but in spite of the attitudes and misinformed opinions of certain people.
I, therefore, respectfully and sincerely ask that Presbytery withdraw the request.

My letter was not answered, nor was I called to any meeting to discuss the matter. The petitioners of Park Street Church were ignored and not given the interview that they had requested. When the trial began three weeks later, I withdrew from preaching. My last sermon was delivered on Sunday, September 20, 1964. The trial opened the next day.

CHAPTER 9

The sequence of hearing, trials, and appeals following my arrest produced in my mind a blurred but macabre kaleidescope of events. Intertwined among strands of truth, whose validity I could recognize, were distortions and lies that I could hardly believe hearing.

Originally, my lawyer, C. E. Perkins, Q.C., planned to have the charges quashed – a legal manoeuvre whereby neither guilt nor innocence is established but the charges themselves are investigated by the Court to see if they have enough weight to warrant a trial. In the first hearing after my arrest the Crown's evidence was quashed as insufficient for trial.

It was the action of the Crown Attorney surrounding this quashed hearing that first alerted us to his desire to obtain a trial and a conviction. Normally, quashed charges are carefully re-examined by the Crown to determine if a case against the accused actually exists. In this instance, the Crown Attorney stood before reporters at the close of the first hearing and stated, "Don't worry, it's not over yet. There'll be new charges or there'll be an appeal."

A few days later, new charges were laid. The Crown Attorney immediately called a press conference and read out the new charges and the information that they were based on. Essentially, they were the same charges together with a few quotations from Crown witnesses. At the same time as the summons was being served on me, I listened to the reports of the press conference on the radio. This questionable procedure was indicative of the Crown's vindictive attitude.

While these preliminary courtroom tactics were underway, my lawyer was engaged in interviews with over 200 people. During this period, we gradually encountered an ever-increasing degree of hostility and obstruction from both the Crown Attorney's office and the Chatham Police Department.

One morning for example, my lawyer received a telephone call that a teen-age girl who was involved in one of the charges and wanted to speak to him; he agreed to see her that afternoon in his office. She didn't keep the appointment; but Mr. Perkins was told by the person who had agreed to drive her to the city that the detective, Tom Bird, had found out what she was about to do and had been instrumental in her not keeping the appointment. He had also threatened the driver with charges if he should try to see her again. The next morning we were before the court, and Mr. Perkins protested this interference with his rights. The Crown Attorney's attitude toward the whole affair was then disclosed when he asked for an order that Mr. Perkins be prevented from speaking to any of the Crown's witnesses; but he refused to say who the Crown's witnesses were. Needless to say the order was not made.

At the next hearing, before Mr. Justice E. L. Haines in Toronto, the Crown's efforts were branded as "weak and flimsy". Mr. Haines ordered the Crown Attorney to provide us with more information about the charges and to allow us sufficient background in the charges to prepare an adequate defence. Specifically, we were to receive copies of all the written statements of the Crown witnesses. The Crown complied with this order, but introduced evidence at the trial that we had never seen and that we had no time to investigate. Our only defence, eventually, was to deny such new evidence.

After months of hearings and pre-trial manoeuvering, we finally stood in a Chatham courtroom faced with eight charges of contributing to juvenile delinquency levelled against me. I began to feel as if the old guard of Park Street United Church stood at the prosecutor's elbow. Rumors, innuendo, and irrelevant references were allowed and, before long, I was stripped of my honor and left standing unarmed amid the fury of the accusations whirling about my head. In the fourteen days of trial, innumerable contradictions and unbased accusations were laid against me by the Crown Attorney and his witnesses. In one instance, there are thirty contradictions in forty pages of testimony reported in the trial's transcript!

On my behalf, reputable men and women whose integrity had never been questioned testified about my character and about my program in the church. They were all informed people who had attended many of the events at which I was alleged to have promoted immoral juvenile sexual behavior. Young people who were a part of the planning, the execution, and the supervision of these events at the church were also witnesses for the defence.

Throughout my trial, my lawyer's confidence in our success was high. He felt that both the background and the stories of the youths testifying for the Crown were among our strongest weapons. They had histories of delinquent behavior. Their testimonies were contradictory and uncorroborated. As we went over our strategy, he noted that each charge was weakly presented and strongly contradicted. I shared his hopes and enthusiasm fully.

Finally, as the judge began to read his decision, we knew it was over. He had not been citing his summary of the trial for more than two minutes when I realized that, despite our efforts, he had decided against us. Shocked, I glanced at my lawyer. He had been confident from the outset that we had the strongest case. He was stunned. Knowing of the events surrounding the allegations, seeing the weakness of the Crown's case, and sharing Mr. Perkin's confidence, I could not accept that the judge had found me guilty. The Crown's case had rested on innuendo, inconsistent and uncorroborated evidence. The judge had accepted it. We had pointed to the contradictions, objected to the oblique attacks of rumor, and presented testimony from adults and youths who had been unchallenged by the Crown. The judge dismissed these efforts.

CHAPTER 10

After I was convicted, I wrote my church officials as follows:

Dear Friends:

Please accept my resignation as minister of Park Street United Church as of this date. Notwithstanding the events of yesterday, I assure you that I am innocent of all the charges brought against me. The judge so found in 15 of the 24 alleged acts and steps have been taken to appeal his findings in the remaining allegations. My faith in God is not shaken and I am certain that justice will eventually triumph. I am grateful for the support both spiritual and material, which I have received from the congregation, and may God bestow His richest blessings upon you. I would respectfully request your prayerful remembrance of me in the hour of my tribulation.

Even my resignation did not still the storm. Indeed, attempts to harass me continued more viciously than ever. I once again received a barrage of obscene phone calls. My anonymous callers branded me a disgrace to the cloth, a Nazi rat, and other unspeakable names. "There's a group of us who are going to get you no matter where you go," was a threat hurled many times. There was a consuming desire on the part of the old guard to get me out of the manse as soon as possible, to keep me off church premises, and to force me from the city. The

Executive of Kent Presbytery made it plain that they condoned this strategy.

The handling of my legal fees indicates the Presbytery's mind at that time. Five months after the Board promised to pay these costs they backed down and reversed this decision. Presbytery then wrote the Board, condoning this action, and their appointed representative in a radio broadcast congratulated Board members on "this demonstration of good churchmanship".

That night when the decision was reversed, the press came to me for my reaction. I said that I was shocked and indignant that the Board's word was not kept, and I termed the action "unethical". Presbytery took me to task for this. Their representative warned that I had greatly harmed my cause by speaking to reporters. I could not understand this attitude. If they thought their action was Christian, should they worry if my feelings were shouted from the housetops?

Some Board members felt the issue had been deliberately clouded; it is hard to come to any other conclusion. The recommendation not to pay the legal fees had been brought to the Board by a small committee selected by Presbytery's ministerial representative. I know that many of its members did not agree with the recommendation. This committee further recommended that my salary be paid to the end of the year, another month. The impression was given that this would be as helpful to me as the paying of lawyer's fees; it was not pointed out, however, that my monthly salary was $400., a far cry from the $8,000 I needed to pay my lawyer. Most of all, these members were grieved that the church dishonored its own word without a second thought and, in doing so, had the connivance of a church court.

Public hostility to this was strong, as shown in numerous letters that reached both my lawyer and me within the next few days. Typical is this one from a former Waterloo parishioner:

Enclosed find my cheque for $100 to help pay for your court expenses. I have made many mistakes but I have never broken a promise. I think the members of Park Street United Church *who agreed to assist you have now given you an unkind deal. I went to Chatham as a bride, years ago, and apparently it hasn't changed since I lived there.*

I wrote these lines to the Presbytery representative who chaired the meeting at which the fee decision was reversed:

Dear. . . . .

In the light of your comments as reported on the radio that the Board of Park Street United Church on December 1st last, demonstrated good churchmanship, and that the reversed decision is not unethical, I feel compelled as a believer in the teachings of Christ to write to you, and in the interests of the church, its witness among men and its future place in our society, to make my strong exception to your opinion of the ethics of this matter known to the officials of the United Church of Canada.

A full disclosure of all the facts concerning the two resolutions discloses, I submit, a complete absence of the most basic Christian principles in the action taken by the Board under your guidance as Interim Moderator on December 1, 1964. This action is particularly confusing to me because of the undertaking which you made to me and to my counsel in my presence that the motion of the Board (to pay the fees) of July 6th, 1964, would be upheld.

The motion of July 6th, 1964, reads as follows: Motion by . . . . that the church meet all legal fees incurred. . . Seconded by . . . . Carried 35 for, 32 against.

The resolution of December 1st, 1964, reads as follows: Whereas there is a strong difference of opinion within the Official Board and the Park Street congregation, and Whereas one of the contentious factors causing this difference concerns the paying of the legal fees for the defence of the Rev. R. D. Horsburgh in his recent court case, and Whereas the church suffers a serious financial crisis, at the moment, and Whereas the payment of the legal fees would increase the

division of the Official Board and the congregation, and
Whereas the people of Park Street Church may voluntarily contribute to the payment of legal fees either through the fund as represented by concerned businessmen of Chatham, as set up for the said purpose, and
Whereas the aim of the Official Board is to dissolve the strong differences of opinion in the light of the question "What is best for Park Street United Church?"
Be it resolved that no action be taken in the matter of payment of the Rev. R. D. Horsburgh's legal fees (As decided at the Board meeting of July 6, 1964) but that Mr. Horsburgh's salary be paid to December 1, 1964.

The Secretary of the Official Board delivered to me a copy of the motion of July 6, 1964. From that action I received a sense of support and financial security in my difficulties. On the basis of that motion I incurred the necessary expenses of my defence without seeking assistance from legal aid or any emergency fund of the United Church of Canada, which would have been necessary, since my salary has never been sufficiently large for me to have any appreciable savings.

I have never been advised officially of the action of the Board on December 1, 1964, although I have seen the copy of the resolution which you gave to my counsel when he attended at your office as a result of the publicity given to the action of the Board on December 1, 1964.

The preamble to that resolution seeks to apply the philosophical concept that the end justifies the means, which is foreign to any interpretation of Christian faith that I have ever heard. The futility of such an idea is evident in the deepening of the division in the congregation which has occurred since the resolution of December 1.

The next matter referred to in the preamble to the resolution is the "serious financial crisis" which the church faces. This is a half truth. As you must know there is a deficit in the operating account of several thousand dollars, but there is no other indebtedness, and at the same time the trustees hold as investments in excess of twenty-five to thirty thousand dollars which are not subject to any direction or limitation as to their use or application.

And finally, the resolution itself, acknowledging the motion of July 6, 1964, and consequently the indebtedness thereby created, does not rescind the motion of July 6th, but merely resolves to take no action to fulfill the obligation. This displays a lack of courage and at the same time demonstrates the completely unethical attitude that the official Board of Park Street United Church does not consider it necessary to meet its obligations, and is not concerned whether its word given on July 6th, 1964, was worthy of belief.

Reference was made in the resolution to the fund started by local business men who are outside the church, to pay for the appeal. This action has been most gratifying to me, but it does not meet the costs of the trial and will not meet all the costs of the appeal. I have received an account for the costs of the trial in the amount of $8,027.08 including fees and disbursements. On this account, I have with the help of several friends, been able to pay the sum of $760.00. I am independently advised that the counsel fee charged me is approximately one-half of what my counsel should receive for the services which he has rendered, and I have only been able to pay about one half of his disbursements on my behalf. I am sure that you can appreciate my great concern in this regard.

I do not believe that the majority of the members of Park Street United Church, if they were fully aware of the facts, would wish to associate themselves with the resolution of December 1, 1964, since the very genius of Christianity is that the welfare of the individual is paramount to the institution.

I trust that you will give the action of the Official Board of Park Street United Church your prayerful reconsideration, and I would ask that you cause the Board of the Church to either rescind the motion of July 6th, 1964 or to pay the account as they have undertaken, so that if necessary the matter may be referred to the higher courts of the church.

Sincerely yours,
R. D. Horsburgh

Presbytery's unethical disposal of my legal fees was most disheartening. I had received no communication from this group other than a cold, formal letter that expressed no concern or even more than polite interest. In answer to a phone call, I went to a meeting of a Presbytery committee called to discuss my present and future welfare. It did not even open or close with prayer, avoiding the usual custom. It dealt only with the most trivial matters.

First of all, they wanted me to leave the manse as soon as possible. They admitted they were being pressured in this matter by my opponents in Park Street Church.

They wanted me to stay off the church premises.

They wanted me to leave Chatham.

They were worried about the book that the Rev. Ronald Smeaton was writing about my case and hoped it would be cleared through the United Church before publication.

Only one question was asked about my financial needs. "Do you think you have enough rapport with the ministers of London Conference that a collection on your behalf would bring response?" the secretary of Presbytery inquired. I answered that I did not know, and the matter was dropped. Not a word about legal costs.

I agreed to leave the manse as soon as possible, this in spite of the fact that the Committee of Stewards had said I could stay there as long as I needed to.

I would not, however, promise to stay entirely away from Park Street United Church, although I assured them that I would be most discreet in my relationship. After all, the church was the one place where I should be welcome. If I were as bad as these people obviously felt, surely the church would be eager to offer me the gospel of redemption of which they are custodians. To this day, however, they have made no attempt to do so, not even offering their ministry of compassion.

I refused emphatically to leave the city, saying that I intended to be cleared on the very ground on which I had been incriminated. It would have been foolish to have left then.

Moreover, I was under instructions from my legal counsel to remain in Chatham, and Presbytery knew this. Indeed, later developments and events justified my staying there.

I said nothing about the church's contemplated "inspection" of Smeaton's book, except to give the name of a possible publisher when asked for it. I knew then that Mr. Smeaton was collaborating with one of Canada's leading lawyers, and I doubted if either of them would submit to censorship by the church.

I left that meeting more disheartened than ever. Presbytery concluded that I would not co-operate and that there was nothing the church could do to help me. On the contrary, I was quite willing to co-operate with Presbytery if their demands were reasonable. I truly believe that Presbytery had every opportunity to give constructive help. I was facing stark poverty at the time. Other groups came to assist me. Why not Presbytery? I believe that prejudice and gossip blinded their eyes to their Christian responsibility and they chose deliberately to pass by on the other side. And I further believe that there is no excuse for their action. I was not to hear from this group again.

Some few days later it became necessary for me to write once more to Presbytery in an attempt to clarify the stand that they had taken from the beginning. My letter was directed to their official representative:

When I was charged Presbytery did not officially offer any assistance. Indeed you and one other minister were the only two members of the clergy of Presbytery who came to me. Your personal contact and offer of assistance was greatly appreciated. As at that time I believed your interest and concern to be for Christian principle.

I decided at that time since I was not guilty of the charges, I would not act as though I were guilty. The Presbytery might have officially offered assistance and taken charge of my congregation, but they did nothing, and as you know there were some members of Presbytery who wanted me defrocked without any trial.

I now sense that during and since the trial, your co-operation has consisted in a behind-the-scenes effort to expel me from the manse and church premises and even the city. Why? Is this Christianity? Cannot the most troubled member seek the sanctuary of his own church?

I always felt that it was not ethical for me to mention this, but at this time I might as well be frank. I believe that if the Christian attitude had been upheld, my salary (perhaps on a minimum basis) would have been protected until after the appeal, and I might have been allowed to remain in the manse for a longer time.

I am grateful that my supporters in the church came to my aid in providing accommodation free of charge. I am subsisting now largely on the voluntary contributions that they have made toward my support. So far as you, your committee, and Presbytery are concerned, my personal welfare has been your least concern. Why ? ? ?

Let us be frank. Does it not seem that you have approached this entire matter on the basis that I must be sacrificed so that the will of a certain group who have always opposed me and former ministers, should prevail? The re-entry of this group into control of the church you have interpreted as church unity. Do you really believe this?

Has this group not attempted to sweep all my rights under the rug because any recognition of those rights would trouble their interpretation of church unity? I contend that they are getting your whole-hearted support. Why ? ?

Christianity is a philosophy on which a man should base his life; it is not a procedure to maintain and enhance the United Church of Canada or any other organization.

It appears to me that you believe that those who supported my program and who formed the majority of the regular attending, contributing, and working members of the church must either change their thinking or be sacrificed with me.

Do you really believe that a church controlled by those who would exclude colored people from their membership, who would deny the facilities of their church to those who have broken the law or come from broken homes, who would withdraw their financial support because they disagree with a majority vote on a program, and that would break a pledge such as the one they undertook – do you really believe that such a church can prosper?

One mother has expressed the depth of the sacrifice that she believes is now being made in Park Street Church. She said (as reported in the Toronto paper) that she had taught her children that a pledge or a promise was sacred and should be kept. Now what can she tell them? The church that proclaims this principle does not uphold it.

I know that some would excuse this by saying the first meeting was illegal. Was it illegal? Let's be honest and straight-forward – the meeting was properly called and properly held; but the results of that meeting offended those who would defeat the purpose of the church – those who have made trouble for ministers before me.

Can you with a clear conscience sacrifice people like that mother who have a real sense of spiritual values and who want to uphold the Christian point of view?

I respectfully request that you comply with my original desire to have Park Street Church either rescind or fulfill the motion of July 6th, 1964, thus leaving me free to take whatever ensuing action is necessary.

Yours sincerely,
R. D. Horsburgh

To this day I have had no reply and the motion has, as yet, neither been fulfilled nor rescinded.

Presbytery's attitude from the beginning showed in the ugly rumors some of its members gleefully countenanced before and after my trial. Not only did I suffer from false witness in court but also from slanderous gossip spread by my brother ministers of the Presbytery, as evidenced by this affidavit sworn before my lawyer and signed by a lay member of the Kent County Boys' Work Board:

Dominion of Canada

Province of Ontario County of Kent To Wit:	**In the matter of** the conduct of the Rev. .... and others as Ministers of the United Church of Canada.

I, ... of the Township of Harwich, in the County of Kent, Farmer,

Do solemnly declare that:

1. I am presently chairman of the Kent County Boys' Work Board and a member of the congregation of the .... United Church charge in the County of Kent.

2. The Kent Boys' Work Board were advised that it was the policy of the United Church of Canada to gradually eliminate interdenominational groups from their camps and for that reason our Board decided not to use Kenesserie Camp in 1964 and we rented the camp site of the Latter Day Saints at Erie Beach, Ontario.

3. At a meeting on our charge in early April of 1964 at which matters concerning Christian Education were being discussed, but which meeting was not involved directly with the Boys' Work Board, the ...., the minister of .... United Church charge, which is adjacent to the City of Chatham, advised the meeting, which was attended by approximately 8 persons that he couldn't understand how the Kent Boys' Work Board could consider the Rev. R. D. Horsburgh as a director of their camp because he was a homosexual, he stated that this was a known fact in Presbytery and that one conference of the United Church of Canada had spent "thousands" trying to have him removed from the ministry. One of the persons attending the meeting asked Mr. .... to cease this discussion because he felt it very improper.

4. One or two days after the said meeting, Rev. .... and Rev. .... of the .... United Church Charge, purporting to represent the Board of Kenesserie United Church Camp

came to my home and requested an immediate decision by the Kent Boys' Work Board as to whether or not they would use Kenesserie Camp for one camp period. Mr. .... said that we might use the camp site if Mr. .... were the director and he repeated the accusations which he previously made against Rev. R. Horsburgh. I asked the Rev. .... if these accusations were true and he replied that "it was" and "it is common knowledge in Presbytery".

5. The Kent Boys' Work Board decided to proceed with their original plans and when the announcement of the camps appeared in the Chatham paper, the Rev. .... came to me and asked that the Board reconsider its decision and cancel its camps. He said if I thought he was "handing me a line" I should call the Rev. .... of .... United Church in Chatham, the Rev. .... of Blenheim, the Rev. .... of Wallaceburg or the Rev. .... as they all knew about it.

6. On the evening of June 29, 1964 when the arrest of the Rev. R. Horsburgh on a charge under the Juvenile Delinquents Act was made known I called the Rev. .... to see whether Presbytery might do anything which would affect our camp with Rev. R. Horsburgh as a director and he advised me that in his opinion Presbytery would not involve itself in any way. He asked me why the Boys' Work Board had kept Mr. Horsburgh as a director since we had surely heard the rumors about him and he suggested that we should cancel the camp and see if the Registrar of the Kent Presbytery Boys' Camp could work our boys into their camp. He further said that it was ridiculous for us to consider carrying on since our camp was only two days off and no parent would let their child attend a camp where a man charged with a moral's offence was a director.

7. In spite of this advice we did carry on with the Rev. R. Horsburgh as director in charge of religious training and ...., the Mayor of Ridgetown, as senior director.

Of the eighty-four boys registered for the camp we had only one cancellation and that one was because the boy was recovering from the mumps.

It is my opinion that the direct statements of Messrs. ...... and the inferences to be drawn from the comments of Mr. ....

were not based on truth, or proven fact and were most Unchristian and improper, particularly when made by one minister of the church about a brother minister.

And I make this solemn declaration conscientiously believing it to be true and knowing that it is of the same force and effect as if made under oath, and by virtue of the Canada Evidence Act.

DECLARED before me at the City
of Chatham in the County of Kent
this 23rd day of July, A.D.
1964.

A COMMISSIONER, ETC.

These damning pieces of gossip, which could be traced back through the years, were being passed around a few weeks before the investigation began. That they added fuel to fire there can be little doubt. In fact, the trial was held in an atmosphere of gossip-mongering. The prosecutor larded his remarks within the context of the trial with this gossip and employed again and again the devious tactic of innuendo.

To answer my accusers, I volunteered to submit to full psychiatric examination. Accordingly, I went to Dr. Alexander Szatmari, neuro-consultant at the Ontario Hospital in Toronto and clinical teacher at the School of Medicine at the University of Toronto. I was guaranteed exhaustive, rigorous tests with emphasis on sexual deviations, and for these I was referred to Douglas Quirk, chief psychologist at the Ontario Hospital, followed by a further examination by Dr. Szatmari. The pertinent parts of the reports given by Dr. Szatmari (a) and Mr. D. Quirk (b) to my lawyer follow:

(a) I should like to point out first, that from my examination, I found the patient neurologically normal, nor could I find any major psychiatric symptomatology. His intelligence is intact, he does not show any organic brain syndrome. What I could detect, is an underlying depression and anxiety. This latter not to be confused with fear of reality, for what I called anxiety in the patient, can be triggered by any traumatic event. *I paid particular attention to any possible sexual aberration, but I could not find any, neither could I detect homosexual or voyeuristic tendencies.*

I referred him for psychological testing to Mr. D. Quirk, our chief psychologist at the Ontario Hospital. Such test would always demonstrate the crystallization forms, because it is a projective test; any kind of sexual deviation can be detected through it. As you will see from the attached copy, none is present. I would strongly point to the last paragraph.

(b) The personality is basically an obsessive one, of the type and motivational character which is well-suited to the ministry – even to having all the original responses which are popular among ministers on the Rorschach. The energy available for effective compensatory or sublimitive use in work is excellent – achieving a maximum score (20) in the 'total' personality area of the DDT. This means that, although he is fairly depressed, he has not decompensated. In the existing obsessive syndrome, the controls over hostile impulses are well balanced, mostly being of a flexible, intellectual variety, which, however, do not permit escape of any real or direct expression of these needs. Reaction formation defenses have converted the energy of assertive impulse into socialized needs for warmth and friendliness and the desire to be liked. These latter manifestations are expressed somewhat in terms of more unconscious controls, referable to his earlier years. This last set of observations indicates that there is a potential for strong control over the closeness needs ('ch' dynamics) which probably got reworked in his early adulthood, as, perhaps, when he entered the ministry.

The present condition, which has been superimposed upon the obsessive personality pattern, and has required further control over his assertive needs, is a depressive reaction – probably to his present life circumstances. However, his stress tolerance remains good, and all that seems to have happened, in general, is that his productivity has been reduced somewhat. On the basis of the test performance, his statement about himself is very likely true: "I have been tremendously enthusiastic in my profession. I have found it to be exceedingly creative and rewarding. I could not have been happier. Of course, there are experiences that can be frustrating, but there are so many compensations. I have had boundless energy – never seem to get tired – and I am physically fit at all times." In his more depressed state, his emotional responsiveness, and his 'boundless energy' have been reduced considerably. Of course, this is just as well, since if he had not withdrawn his emotional cathexes, there would, of course, have been a risk of suicide (i.e., the symbolic act of destroying emotionality). As things stand, I would think that the prognosis would be quite good, once he has a chance to re-invest his energies in a new life.

The crucial questions which I gather are at stake here, and which I am called upon to provide an answer to, are questions concerning his psychosexual mode of adjustment. At the deep layer of organization, the dynamics are the dynamics of an obsessive personality, oriented toward helping others by reaction formation. This is an ethical solution to the genital problem. At a more surface level, largely on a reactive basis, there is the expectation of sadistic attack from his life space (an expectation obviously based on current events), and a compulsive concern about himself which expresses itself mildly, (as an obvious set of doubts about himself engendered by present life circumstances – it is a shame that we humans can be aroused to such self-doubts, but of course, this is the nature of reactive depressions). In sum, however, there *is absolutely no evidence of any of the kinds of perversions which are commonly frowned upon in our society. There is no indication whatsoever of homosexuality, or of paedophilia, or of hyper-genitality, or of voyeurism or exhibitionism. The overall functioning is well within normal limits.*

CHAPTER 11

"YOU ARE A TERRIBLE MAN. YOU SHOULD BE TARRED AND FEATHERED. MAY YOUR SOUL BURN IN HELL."

That was a letter I received; but not the worst. Some went to my lawyer. Others went to those who set up legal aid funds and prayer chains. Most anonymous letters were unspeakably foul, and all in the name of Christianity. Most anonymous writers seemed eager to boast that they were Christian. A minister blushed when I showed him some of the letters. "Surely," he said, shocked, "no Christian would write stuff like this." I replied, "I think it's a cinch no atheist wrote it."

There were such messages as, "Satan has a home for you. I hope you burn in hell and your supporters with you." One "Christian" ended a raving, ranting letter, "Where are all the keys and locks on the doors of the church? It's a wonder we have any church left. May God punish you for your sins." Another wrote, "I hope your lawyer loses his practice defending a Nazi rat like you."

Perhaps it's significant to note that most of these anonymous letters left much to be desired in spelling and grammar. A few striking examples are: "tared" for "tarred", "fethered" for "feathered," and "Satin" for "Satan".

On the other hand, thousands of people wrote letters assuring me of their faith and support. The first strong words of encouragement after my arrest came from a rabbi:

Dear Rev. Horsburgh: In your mental anguish and disillusionment, it should be fortifying to know that so many members of your congregation stand at your side. A host of friends beyond the confines of your community also have a deep and undiminished faith in you. Among these, I want to express to you an intense feeling of sympathy and regard, and of hope that you will finally triumph over this crisis in your life and career. May God grant you the strength and unconquerable self-confidence to shape your agony into ever wider service to Him and to mankind, and may He vouchsafe the grace of insight and wisdom to your people.

An Anglican Rector wrote,

I have deliberately not read the accounts of the Horsburgh affair in the newspapers for I feel they are playing the sensational aspect far too much. Instead of trying to seek truth and see what you were endeavoring to accomplish with teen-agers they simply word their articles to sell newspapers. I sincerely hope the outcome of your trial will be in your favor. I cannot help but feel that you have been the whipping-boy for the failure of many adults in Chatham and indeed of our sick society in general. May your faith in God continue to carry you forward. The Church members are in error, but not the Christian faith.

From a Presbyterian minister,

Some of us have suffered in the ministry along lines that have a close relationship to your trouble. My particular interest in you had come after I have been given the grace to discredit so much of the wrong that has been said from sources I deemed reliable.

A Congregational minister in the United States wrote,

The injustice of the whole business is outrageous. How could the testimony of children known to be evil, on probation, in reformatories, etc., be taken against that of ministers and godly laymen?

From a layman,

I am satisfied that my words express the thoughts of thousands. You may have been too trusting but I am convinced that your endeavors were misunderstood. The fact that you could have everything to lose and nothing whatever to gain if the charges were true confirms me in my conviction. Thus, I am exceedingly surprised that your torment even started, let alone continues unabated. May I assure you that, public reports notwithstanding, you have thousands of unknown friends who sympathize with you in your time of trouble.

From another,

I was shocked to pick up the newspaper last night and read about charges against you, but I was not surprised. People who do things receive a great deal of attention and criticism. The prudent course is to follow the familiar pattern set by the ages. With the prudent course there can be no progress. People who have convictions cannot be prudent. Socrates, Christ, Galileo, Darwin, Joan of Arc, and thousands of others with convictions had to face trial and persecution because of those convictions. The ages exonerate those pioneer thinkers who are condemned by their contemporaries. Time is on your side. It is on the side of every person who has convictions based on truth. Your work with the young people of Chatham may have rescued from disaster a person whose future course and action may benefit all mankind. That you may know the result of your work matters little. What you did, you did because God told you it was the right thing to do. He cannot be wrong.

Young people in all my congregations were numerous in the ranks of enthusiastic letter-writers. One young woman from Zion United Church, Hamilton, wrote,

I refuse to believe that you are guilty of any of those charges. Let us know if we, the young people of Zion, can do anything for you. You did a great good here. I have already talked to many and they wish to help. We are willing to sign a petition, or come up in full force.

From a school teacher who had grown up in Zion Church

and who later attended my church in Waterloo while at University there:

Somehow with all the trials and tribulations you've encountered while making your ministry meaningful, you've always managed to come out on top. I expect the results of these painful times will be no exception. In the estimation of your many hundreds of friends, your integrity is beyond reproach. The contribution you have made to the wholesomeness of mind and body of today's youth is beyond evaluation. During the 13 years we have been friends, you have undoubtedly been one of the chief influences of my life. God speed the inevitable result.

From another young man came these stirring words:

Having lived in Chatham and being a close associate of yours in Waterloo, I feel I have a better grasp of the issue than most. I see behind the facade of morality that this case supposedly stood for. The bigotry, selfishness, small-mindedness of the church board (or at least many of them) was quite evident to me in Waterloo as well as Chatham. We both knew that a clash was coming but one of such devious and Machiavellian structure was hard to visualize.

Young people I hadn't heard from in years made contact:

I remember the many fine times I spent with you in Westdale United Church in Hamilton 18 years ago. I feel I should let you know that one of the thousands of young people with whom you have worked during your life has not forgotten you and still holds you in the highest regard. I know from personal experience how you feel about young people and certainly trust that you will continue to help them in the future as you have done in the past.

The fact that many practising Christians don't attend church is testified to in many letters from good people who make religion a daily affair and who, unlike so many of my detractors, hew to their faith seven days a week. Typical of these is the following:

I find it hard to think that you are being confronted with a court case because your efforts to help young people were too vigorous. It is even more discouraging if the information against you grew out of resentment against some other steps you took in your ministry. I am no longer a Christian, nor in fact am I interested in any church as an adherent. But I think I understand what you and others like you are trying to accomplish when you take steps to move the church from its complete emphasis on imposing edifices and reassuring but meaningless services which never offend to playing a vital part in contending with the social problems we face today. I think the attempts you have made represent the only possible direction the church can go if it is to remain at all viable as an institution.

The encouragement of these and other letters convinced me that the general public did not condemn me but easily recognized there was more to the matter than appeared in hysterical newspaper reports. Before the curtain fell, thousands of letters came from Canada, the United States, England, Europe, Africa, Pakistan, and Australia. My desk was buried in letters, the first lapping of support that surged in for two years. Even now, the heartening ripples of encouragement still reach me from many parts of the world.

How will I ever make known the gratitude I feel for the many who stood by me with such unflinching faith? Only a minority ostracized me. Unfortunately some were among the clergy of my own presbytery and city. I am grateful to those who were not afraid to come forward to support me in a city charged with hate and vindictiveness; but I fail to understand those who did not come at all or who came only to give advice which I could not always in good conscience take and who as a result, deserted my side. In truth, of course, no one can really help in a time of crisis. Man must carry his agony alone. He must climb the mountain of thought, away from the medley of voices, and, with God's help, come to peace. An old Negro spiritual expresses that loneliness so simply:

You've got to cross that lonesome valley,
You've got to cross it for yourself.
There ain't no one gonna cross it for you,
You've got to cross it for yourself.

CHAPTER 12

Looking back at the trial, I see three areas in which I was defeated and upon which I was convicted: the pressures of the Chatham Police Department on the young witnesses, the blasé indifference of the Crown Attorney to the question of justice, and the receptiveness of these youths to pressure from the Crown and police.

Throughout the accounts about each of the Crown witnesses runs the story of efforts by the Chatham Police Department to evince testimony from the young people at all costs. Further statements given to both myself and my lawyer confirm these descriptions of police pressures.

Several Crown witnesses were awaiting legal actions for their own misdemeanors. One young man was under a charge of rape. It was never mentioned during the course of my trial. One girl was promised a shortened reformatory term, which she was serving for unmanageability at the time of my trial. Another boy was waiting to be charged for theft. These charges, or the vulnerable position that the young people were in while shadowed by the charges, gave police a great deal of room for pressure.

Several of those who were not charged were under pressure to testify for the Crown. Others wanted to change their stories but were told that if they did so, they could be charged with obstructing justice.

Whenever police pressure was mentioned, the young persons involved spoke of harassing interviews with the police, often in front of parents and including statements of personal involvement in the sexual activities alleged to have occurred. Some of these who later changed their testimony stated that these interviews produced the initial evidence used against me and that they were later reinforced by threats of legal action for obstructing justice.

The second concern that I have as a result of the trial involves the actions of the Crown Attorney's office. During the trial it was evident that the Crown Attorney's first goal was a conviction, not the establishment of the justice of the case. This attitude of mine has not changed; in fact, subsequent events strengthened it.

During the appeal, my lawyer, Charles Dubin, accused the Crown Attorney of employing innuendo, gossip, and rumor as evidence. The Crown Attorney also distorted the truth by omission of important facts. One example of this suffices.

The prosecutor, in his summary, told the judge that one witness testified that I had opened the door to the church parlor to watch a couple have sexual intercourse. In fact, the witness had said that I had opened the door and had seen one couple in an incriminating position on a chesterfield. Both the witness and the Crown knew more about those circumstances than they admitted.

As each of them knew, those young people had permission to use the church parlor on Sunday afternoons to listen to records. One provision of this privilege included the keeping of the door open. On this occasion, I happened to walk past the parlor with the Crown witness, saw the door closed and opened it. Inside, the young people – four or five of them – were lounging about and behaving quite properly. The Crown Attorney asked nothing about the witness's idea of an incriminating position. He did not ask the witness specifically if the young people were engaged in sexual intercourse. The witness did not say that they were engaged in sexual intercourse. The Crown encouraged no specific information from him about the circumstances. In his summation, the Crown stated emphatically that the couple were engaged in intercourse. This was typical of the Crown's attack.

The evidence for all eight charges was flimsy in the extreme, as Mr. Justice Haines stated early in the proceedings. It is impossible to resist the conclusion that the reason the Crown amassed so many charges against me was the belief that the more mud thrown the more chance there was that some of it would stick. If the prosecution had been confined to three or four charges and restrained from tossing in so much innuendo and rumor it is possible that the judge would have cleared me altogether. As it was, five "guilties" in exchange for three "not guilties" might easily be interpreted as a reasonable exchange, a compromise.

The third area that concerned me involves the witnesses themselves. In fact, in order to gain perspective on all these three issues, we must take a hard look at each of the major Crown witnesses.

The first, a girl, was presented by the Crown as a high example of good character. In fact, she was one of his most questionable witnesses. In a written statement to the police prior to the trial, she claimed to have had sexual relations with two boys at the church. We checked her story with the boys, who were most anxious to deny it and to persuade the girl to tell the truth. They insist to this day that she was lying.

The first of these boys telephoned her and invited me to listen to the conversation on the extension. I felt that the conversation warranted recording. Here is the precise dialogue:

BOY: What's this I hear about you telling the cops Mr. Horsburgh gave us permission to use the church apartment for intercourse? You know he didn't.

GIRL: I know he didn't.

BOY: Well, what are you saying he did for?

GIRL: Well, everybody else is against him, aren't you?

BOY: No. I'm not. What would I be against him for?

GIRL: Oh, I thought you were.

BOY: Well, I'm not, and you'd better not drag me in on this or you'll be a dead duck.

GIRL: I won't, I promise.

But in the Courtroom, she testified with poker face and with her mother beside her for moral support that I had permitted the two of them to use the apartment for sexual intercourse. She went so far as to mention the day and the hour when the event occurred. She had positive proof. Fortunately, I was able to prove that I was 350 miles away at the time that she mentioned and was able to produce evidence to this effect. The Crown, however, insisted that the girl was mistaken about the time and that I had been present when they were in the apartment. He was not satisfied that she might be fabricating a story; I had to be guilty. I was acquitted of this charge.

The other boy mentioned in her statement to the police also insisted that the girl was lying. He too telephoned her, and again I listened and recorded their conversation. This time another person, a chaperone at the dance, also listened.

BOY: Why did you tell the police we had intercourse? You know perfectly well we didn't.

GIRL: I know we didn't.

BOY: Well, why did you say we did?

GIRL: I had to say it.

BOY: Well, why?

GIRL: Because the police made me cry in front of my parents and I had to say it.

BOY: You don't usually lie.

GIRL: Well, you've got a point there.

BOY: Aren't you going to tell the truth?

GIRL: I don't know, I think it's too late now.

Once again the girl lied in court. Once again I had evidence that cleared me; but there was no indication that the judge doubted her credibility. In fact, he referred to my testimony as "alibi" evidence.

Another Crown witness was on probation at the time for drinking under age and for unmanageability, and during my trial he was involved in a theft for which he was later given a suspended sentence. It is interesting here to note that the Crown was fully aware of this boy's criminal activity during the course of my trial. In fact, Detective Tom Bird investigated the matter; but neither he nor the Crown would bring the matter into the light until after my trial and conviction were settled! (One can't help but wonder how concerned these men were to see that justice was a primary consideration of that court, although I had really stopped wondering long before!)

For several months this boy's parents had been coming to me to discuss their family problems. They told me many times that they never knew when this boy told the truth. "He so seldom does," the mother said. I advised them to take the problem to a probation officer, and finally the boy was placed on probation. I recall that the parents were profuse in their appreciation of my help. Nevertheless, they upheld their son when he accused me, and the mother was a supporter of the Crown.

This boy had told the police that I had sent him to the church apartment to attack a girl. But some weeks before the trial he told five friends that he lied to the detective "just to get him off my back". His friends came at once to my lawyer and volunteered to swear out affidavits. They were not called to witness at the trial, simply because my lawyer felt that this boy's credibility would not be accepted by the judge under any circumstances. He had an unsavory background and his testimony was not corroborated. His story conflicted on many points with that told by the girl involved. Moreover, a defence witness, a lad of unimpeached character, now a Provincial Police cadet, gave testimony that countered the Crown's evidence; but it was not heeded. I was convicted on this count.

One day, as I was motoring along a Chatham street in company with another United Church minister, I saw a fifteen-year-old boy who later became a third Crown witness. I knew that he had already given a written statement to the police in which he had accused me of permitting and encouraging his sexual delinquency. He waved and we stopped to talk. I asked him about his statement to the police. He flatly denied that he had given any such statement. He denied that I had contributed in any way to his misbehavior. "It was my old lady who said all that to the police," he said. This boy, on probation at the time, later testified against me in court, and, although his testimony was garbled, contradictory, and uncorroborated, I was still convicted on this count.

During the trial a girl, a fourth Crown witness, approached my lawyer at his home and apologized for saying in court that I had condoned her misbehavior in the church. Her belief was that if she would co-operate with the Crown she might be released from the reformatory before Christmas. "I want so badly to be home for Christmas," she said, "I had to say what I did."

A nineteen-year-old youth admitted in court that he carried a forged baptismal certificate. He said he didn't have it with him when he was questioned in court by my lawyer; but later he admitted to the Reverend Ronald Smeaton, author of *The Horsburgh Affair*, and to me that it was in his pocket in court. The judge termed him a reliable witness and said in his judgment, "I accept the testimony of this boy." He, too, had incriminated me in his evidence. Later, this "reliable" witness swore out an affidavit retracting his court testimony.

His girl friend said under oath that she had lied in her written statement to the police and decided to change her story in court. She, too, insisted that I had permitted her misbehavior in church; but at the end of a lengthy cross-examination denied the allegations she had previously made. Nevertheless, I was convicted on her evidence. Some months later she voluntarily came to my lawyer and swore out an affidavit withdrawing her first court story, which incriminated me.

One could go on at length with similar examples, for the

trial transcript is full of them. I have mentioned enough, however, to demonstrate that over the testimony of every Crown witness is a large question-mark.

During the months between trial and appeal, several Crown witnesses came to my lawyer and to me to admit their mistakes and to make amends. One girl wrote a letter: "I feel I was rash and vindictive at the time. I was under pressure from the police and another adult." Another said, "I turned against Mr. Horsburgh to get the heat off myself. I knew I could get into trouble if I didn't pass the buck. That is why we all decided to go against him."

A girl told me that when she was questioned by Detective Bird she said definitely that I had no knowledge of the "affairs" that had been going on. Two days later, however, she met a young man already in the conspiracy and who later became a Crown witness, and he told her that all the young people were going to blame the minister. "They'll do nothing to him," he said, "but we could be in serious trouble." At this, the girl went to the police the next day and changed her story to incriminate me. This time she was supported by her parents who felt she was doing the right thing.

Again, the girl whose telephone denials I had recorded was asked why she blamed the minister and she replied, "Well, everyone else is against him, why shouldn't I be, too?" Several Crown witnesses told us that the police had warned them that if they changed their stories they could be charged with an offense. The youth facing a rape charge at the time of my trial was expecting help with his case if he co-operated in the charges against me.

When Detective Bird learned that these youths were changing their stories, he sought a Crown witness for an interview. This young man reports that he reminded the detective in no uncertain terms that the whole affair was a farce. "You know your investigation was phony," the youth said, "And you know your witnesses lied." He says that the detective replied, "I'll admit Mr. Horsburgh is no criminal, but people do get charged with careless driving. Some people thought there was an undesirable situation at Park Street Church and I had to clean it up. All power to him if he wins his appeal."

Just how completely these Crown witnesses reversed their stories is shown in the following two affidavits sworn out months after the trial in the office of Chatham lawyer William Magee:

Dominion of Canada

Province of Ontario County of Kent of TO WIT	**In the matter of** THE APPEAL OF RUSSELL D. HORSBURGH from his conviction on five counts of contributing to juvenile delinquency, contrary to section 33 (1 (b)) of the Juvenile Delinquents Act.

I, , of the City of Chatham in the County of Kent, Student

Do solemnly declare that:

1. I was one of the witnesses called by the Crown at the trial of the said Russell D. Horsburgh, and I gave evidence on behalf of the Crown concerning several of the acts in the counts of which the accused was found guilty.

2. I correctly described in my evidence occasions on which I had intimate sexual relations with another teenager in the buildings known as Park Street United Church, in the City of Chatham, Ontario, however my evidence at the said trial was not correct wherein I said or inferred that I had told the accused about such sexual relations, or discussed such matters with him, or wherein I indicated that I knew that the accused had any knowledge of these events.

3. The accused on no occasion gave me permission to use any part of the church premises for the purpose of having sexual intercourse, nor has he on any occasion arranged, encouraged or condoned any improper activity on my part.

4. All of the improper activities in which I participated were

conducted in such a manner as to keep any knowledge of them from the accused or any other person, and to prevent the accused, or anyone, from ever suspecting that such improper activities took place, and wherein my evidence at the said trial is to the contrary, my evidence at the said trial was in error.

5. I gave such erroneous evidence at the trial of the accused because I was very angry with the accused since another teenage boy, who was becoming particularly active in the youth groups at the church, was replacing me as an important senior member of such youth groups, and in the affections of my girl friend, and I felt that the accused was somehow responsible for this, although there was not any logical reason for me to so believe.

6. I conspired with Mrs. ...., an adult who subsequently gave evidence for the Crown at the trial of the accused, to provide a newspaper story to publically reveal certain improper conduct by a few teenagers in the buildings of the said church and to involve the accused with this activity in such publicity so that his career would be injured.

7. Prior to giving my testimony at the trial of the accused, and after I revealed to the investigating police officer, my sexual relations with one of the other teenage witnesses for the Crown, I indicated to the said officer, Det. Sgt. ......, that I was afraid of being charged with an offence. He then advised me that there was no interest in charging anyone but the accused, Russell D. Horsburgh, and that if I did not tell the same story at the trial as I had told him, I could be charged with obstructing justice. He further advised me that I could request the protection of the Canada Evidence Act before giving my evidence at the trial. As a result of this advice I was afraid then to truthfully say at the trial of the accused that the accused had no knowledge of, or involvement in the incidents of improper sexual activities about which I gave evidence, and I attempted to so word my evidence at the trial as to infer the involvement of the accused but to leave to me the position of possibly misinterpreting the words or actions of the accused.

8. I am advised by .... (four other Crown witnesses) and I do verily believe that threats and inducements were held out

to them to involve the accused in their testimony at the trial concerning their improper activities in and about the said church buildings.

9. On Sunday June 27th, 1965, I telephoned C. E. Perkins, Q.C., counsel for the accused, and arranged to meet with him, at which meeting I voluntarily, and without inducement or coercion, gave this declaration to correct the errors in my previous testimony since I had come to realize that a great injustice had been done the accused because of such errors in my previous testimony, and my conscience required that I do something to correct the wrong that I had done.

And I make this solemn declaration conscientiously believing it to be true and knowing that it is of the same force and effect as if made under oath, and by virtue of the Canada Evidence Act.

DECLARED before me at the City
of Chatham
in the County
of Kent
this 27th day of June
1965

Dominion of Canada

Province of Ontario of TO WIT	**In the matter of** The Appeal of Russell D. Horsburgh from his conviction on five counts of contributing to Juvenile Delinquency, contrary to section 33 (1 (b)) of the Juvenile Delinquents Act.

I, of the City of Chatham in the County of Kent, Student

Do solemnly declare that:

1. I was one of the witnesses called by the Crown at the trial of Russell D. Horsburgh and I gave evidence concerning several of the counts on which he was found guilty.

2. I was influenced by .... to make statements to the police attributing to Russell D. Horsburgh knowledge of my conduct about the buildings of Park Street United Church which statements were incorrect as was my evidence to the same effect at the trial of Russell D. Horsburgh.

3. The truth of the matter is that I have never heard Mr. Horsburgh talk of sex to me or anyone else, and I believe that Mr. Horsburgh did not know what was going on between my boyfriend and myself while we were in the apartment or parlour of the church.

4. I made a serious mistake in giving false evidence against Mr. Horsburgh, and I have given this declaration voluntarily in the hope of doing something to correct that mistake.

And I make this solemn declaration conscientiously believing it to be true and knowing that it is of the same force and effect as if made under oath, and by virtue of the Canada Evidence Act.

DECLARED before me at the City
of Chatham
in the County
of Kent
this 6th day of September
1965

These affidavits sparked a controversy that was not to end until it reached the floor of the Ontario Legislature.

I was in jail pending leave to appeal when they were sworn out. My lawyer brought them to me late one night. I saw them as clear-cut retractions of court testimony that incriminated me. I asked my lawyer for his reaction. He replied, "They are dynamite!" That night, I was inspired with the high hope that the charge represented by the affidavits would be dropped at once, and that the remaining testimony of Crown witnesses would now be brought to the bar of serious doubt. Imagine my shock when I read some weeks later a report in the *Toronto Telegram* to the effect that the Attorney General interpreted the affidavits not as a *retraction* of court testimony but rather a *modification* of it! I resigned myself to the fact that the fight must go on.

Three years later, when I was free to speak my mind openly without fear of prejudicing my case, I declared in a press interview that I felt the Attorney General's interpretation of the affidavits was not on the side of justice. I believed then, as I do now, that my statement was nothing more than fair comment. But the Attorney General did not agree. In a carefully prepared brief to the Ontario Legislature, he blasted my remarks as "scurrilous" and "mischievous," an aspersion on the administration of law and justice and on his own personal integrity.

In retrospect, these affidavits, although seldom mentioned in appeal courts, nevertheless became a basic issue in the defence that my lawyers used in the case. In fact, they may have been the key to my eventual acquittal.

The affidavits, although they were produced by only two of the key Crown witnesses, stated the sentiments of all the major witnesses. Beyond that, they became a sort of "behind-the-scenes" basis for the legal battles that I was to fight in the next three years. Even today, with the trials and accusations formally dismissed, they represent my first line of defence against the charges, suspicions, and doubting phrases hurled at me from time to time.

After the original trial under Judge William Fox in Chatham, I became involved in three separate appeal trials. The first, in the Supreme Court of Ontario, was heard by Mr. Justice Eric Moorhouse, and it upheld the original convictions. Subsequently, the affidavits were produced and verified by an independent lawyer who had no other connection with my case.

It was at this time that I obtained the services of Mr. Charles Dubin as my counsel. Mr. Dubin's reputation as one of Canada's foremost criminal lawyers had attracted my attention. His performance in the subsequent appeal courts and in my final retrial justified beyond a shadow of a doubt my first hopes with him. I am today very deeply indebted to him for his efforts on my behalf.

In the first appeal, Mr. Justice Moorhouse said that his judgment confirming the conviction was based on the theories that uncorroborated testimony of juveniles is acceptable and that the trial Judge was consistent in his assessment of the credibility of witnesses!

The argument of the defense does not convince me that the learned Judge erred in concluding that corroboration was unnecessary. These witnesses were not under such disability of being regarded as witnesses who could hope to escape from danger hanging over them by giving evidence favourable to the Crown. Indeed it was just the opposite. It is clear he directed his mind to corroboration, having regard both to the nature of the offence and the ages of the witnesses for the prosecution and concludes corroboration is not necessary. . . . .

It was argued before me that the learned Judge's findings on the issue of credibility were inconsistent on the evidence. In my respectful opinion there are few trials where inconsistencies in evidence cannot be found. But in my respectful opinion the question of credibility must be determined by the judicial officer having in mind the whole of the evidence, the manner and demeanour of the witnesses when the evidence was given and I am not satisfied that the learned Judge misdirected himself on any legal principles in that respect.

In the second appeal, a panel of three judges in the Ontario Court of Appeal heard the evidence and again upheld the conviction. In this case, the evidence of the affidavits was not admitted and the majority opinion ruled that the testimony of the witnesses, even though given by juveniles and uncorroborated, was still valid! Mr. Justice Gregory Evans declared that the affidavits should be inadmissible because "there must be some finality to the evidence of a trial" . . .!

Justice Evans stated in his judgment that the main issue in the case was that of credibility:

The learned Court Judge had the opportunity of hearing the witnesses and observing them during the course of their evidence and at trial. The Court of Appeal should not lightly interfere with the findings of a lower court with respect to the issue of credibility and I am satisfied that in the present case there was no fundamental error with respect to the issue of credibility and that the learned Court Judge was correct in accepting the evidence of the Crown witnesses, not all of whom were children, as against the unsupported denial of the accused . . . It is clear that the learned Court Judge made a careful examination of the evidence and the relevant authorities before reaching his decision. I am in agreement with his decision.

Mr. Justice C. J. O. Porter agreed with Justice Evans:

The Juvenile Delinquents Act provides there must be corroboration of the evidence of children of tender years but makes no provision for corroboration otherwise. Corroboration is a statutory safeguard. Since the Act omits to make further provision for corroboration it must be taken to have been intended that corroboration is not necessary. . . .

In my view the learned Juvenile Court Judge examined the evidence with the greatest care, and gave the fullest consideration to all situations in which there was or might have been reasonable doubt.

In a significant dissenting judgment, Mr. Justice Bora Laskin ruled that a mistrial had occurred in Chatham and that the original convictions were not acceptable. The Crown had not proven its case.

Justice Laskin's opinions became the basis for my subsequent appeal to the Supreme Court of Canada and the latter's judgment can only be understood in the light of Mr. Justice Laskin's report:

I address myself, in the main, to two issues that were contested on the appeal: first, whether the law respecting accomplices and the rule of danger of convicting on their uncorroborated evidence applies to juveniles in proceedings under the Juvenile Delinquents Act; and, second, whether, in any event, there is a rule of practice, applicable to charges under the Juvenile Delinquents Act, that it is dangerous to convict on the uncorroborated evidence of complainants in sexual cases. Both the trial Judge and Moorhouse J. held that corroboration was not required and, inferentially, that there was no need to assess the evidence of the juvenile witnesses from the standpoint of any danger of resting a conviction on their evidence alone. I disagree with the views expressed by the Courts below on these matters, and hold, accordingly, that none of the convictions can stand. . . . .

Although an appellate Court is ordinarily entitled to assume that a trial Judge sitting alone would guide himself by the proper standards in dealing with charges supported only by evidence of accomplices, the present case exhibits a clear rejection by the trial Judge of the applicability of any such standards. This defect in his approach to the case before him is not cured by his acceptance of the evidence of the juvenile accomplices in preference to the accused's categorical denials. The balance he struck took no account of the obligation to assess the evidence of the juveniles as being that of accomplices and not of independent witnesses. . . .

I turn to the second issue mentioned above, namely, whether a rule obtains in respect of charges under the Juvenile Delinquents Act that it is dangerous to convict on the uncorroborated evidence of a complainant in a sexual case. . . .

The record of the trial contains no evidence that, in my view, can be called corroborative. However, the fatal flaw in the proceedings below was in the determination that the charges could be disposed of without any regard for the rules of caution, dictated by authority as well as by experience, with which evidence of accomplices and of complainants in sexual cases must be viewed. . . .

Because emphasis was placed by Moorhouse J. as well as by the trial Judge on the issue of credibility, I do not wish to conclude these reasons without commenting on it. . . .

An assessment of credibility which amounts to nothing more than the flat statement by the trial Judge that he believes one witness and disbelieves another may be difficult if not impossible for an appellate Court to review; but it is not a manifestation of the application of any standard of judgment. The trial Judge here did more than this, as his reasons show, but those reasons betray an inconsistency in standards that make some of his conclusions impossible to accept. . . .

Before I give examples I think it important to note that, with one exception, the only sworn evidence found by the trial Judge to be relevant to the charges on which the accused was convicted was that of young people associated in the misconduct to which the accused allegedly contributed. The trial Judge believed them all. Where their stories were inconsistent he chose to believe them anyway, while disbelieving the accused on certain assertions on which he was supported by independent evidence.

One of the independent witnesses who corroborated the accused, . . . the trial Judge described as "intelligent and straightforward." Why was his evidence rejected? Because he was one of a group of young people who participated in a "rough party" in the church premises, staying there for awhile and not telling the accused about it. Why he, rather than any others, should have brought tales to the accused was not disclosed by the trial Judge. [He] was not one of the "roughies," and the trial Judge refers to the fact that [the boy] was shocked by what he saw. Nevertheless, he is dismissed as not a completely candid witness. But [a] 13-year-old [girl] is given credence notwithstanding that she was at the party, kicking around a water-filled rubber contraceptive, and notwithstanding discrepancies between her evidence and that of her sister.

[Another boy] is also believed in preference to the accused notwithstanding that (to use the trial Judge's words) "he did not impress me as being very intelligent. His memory was faulty as far as dates and estimates as to time were concerned. He had little or no recollection of details but was able to recall major and unusual events. . . ." So far as appears from the transcript and from the trial Judge's review, the major events in the life of this boy, who had reached only grade 7 at 16 years of age, were his acts of intercourse with [his girl friend]. The trial Judge also adds that this witness was confused at times. But he is fully credited. And he is credited against the accused's denial by a finding of the trial Judge that is wrong as a matter of law. . . .

[The girl's] mother testified she was unmanageable. The girl uttered a vulgarity in Court. She had sexual intercourse in the church on her first visit there, being brought by [a boy] who wanted to talk to the accused about marriage with her. They had intercourse again. The trial Judge, in assessing the credibility of [these two], puts this question to himself: Why would these youngsters tell the story they did tell about the accused if it was not true? Surely, the answer is obvious, and it confirms the wisdom of the rules of caution that I considered earlier in these reasons.

The trial Judge adopted a somewhat similar method of assessing . . . a girl whose promiscuity at age 15 is spread upon the record. [A boy] under probation at the material time, and a boy who on the evidence forced intercourse upon [a girl], is accepted as a fully creditable witness. The conduct of all the young witnesses in their misbehaviour on church property, was disgraceful, but the accused cannot be held responsible for it merely because it occurred there, or because he provided the opportunity through the programme of activities which he carried on at the church. If the church did allow its range of activities to outrun necessary provision for supervision, the results shown by the evidence herein must compel sober reassessment.

I have one final observation on the matter of credibility. The accused put his character in issue by calling a large number of character witnesses, reputable persons who testified to the accused's good reputation and good work. It is a fact that this evidence goes only to June, 1960, which is before the accused came to Chatham. But it stood unimpeached by the Crown. There is not one word about it in the trial Judge's reasons, either in terms of reliability or of weight. It was entitled to consideration and I consider it prejudicial error to ignore it. . . .

Since in my opinion none of the convictions can stand, it remains to determine whether a new trial should be ordered or an acquittal directed. The offences with which the accused is charged are triable before a Judge alone, and I do not think that a legally trained trier of fact, on a proper application of the rules of evidence to the testimony adduced herein, could find the Crown's case proved beyond a reasonable doubt. I would therefore direct an acquittal.

Throughout both appeals, my lawyers had followed a basic defence that centred on fourteen simple points. They claimed that, even without the affidavits, there was sufficient evidence available to warrant dismissal of the charges.

Essentially, Mr. Dubin, my chief counsel, argued that the decision of the judge was against the weight of evidence and the law; that the charges were void for duplicity and uncertainty, and failure to identify acts clearly so that a full and adequate defence could be prepared; that the judge erred in deciding the Crown had complied with an order from Mr. Justice E. L. Haines to supply the defence with full particulars; that the judge erred in allowing children of tender years to be sworn; that he misdirected himself in his test of their credibility.

Other grounds were that Judge Fox erred in allowing the Crown to amend its information at the end of its case, had erred in trying me on all eight counts together, and had failed to consider the uncontroverted evidence, which weighed heavily in my favor.

The application said that the judge's findings on the issue of credibility of witnesses was inconsistent and the evidence on which I was convicted "was demonstrably incapable of belief and no judge properly directing himself as to law could accept such evidence."

The judge had also erred in stating that unless I could show that the Crown witnesses had a motive for lying, their evidence would be accepted.

With the two unsuccessful forays into the Ontario Courts of Appeal behind us, we turned to the Supreme Court of Canada. Three issues were instrumental in the acceptance of the appeal by the Supreme Court of Canada. First, the judgment of Mr. Justice Laskin added great weight to our claim that, in both substance and procedure, the original trial had been improper. Secondly, the fourteen points were taken as indications of possible misconduct in the Chatham proceedings. Finally, the affidavits were accepted.

In their majority opinion, the Supreme Court of Canada ruled that a mistrial had taken place in Chatham. They ordered a new hearing.

They based their conclusions on the fourteen points introduced by the defence. These points were made more reasonable by:

1 Mr. Justice Laskin's opinions,
2 the weight of character evidence on my behalf,
3 the error of the judge in applying the rules properly,
4 the two affidavits.

Setting out the general tone of the Supreme Court's favorable judgment, Mr. Justice Markland's summary is most explicit. His statement spoke for the majority who favored granting the appeal for a new trial:

The accused is a married man, 45 years of age who has been an ordained minister since 1947, following the completion of his education at McMaster University where he obtained a B.A. degree and Queen's University where he earned a divinity degree. He came to a Chatham pastorate after previous service in Creighton Mine, Sudbury, Hamilton, and Waterloo. The offences of which he was convicted had as their locale the Church in Chatham at which he served, and an apartment attached to the church which was not inhabited but was used as a collection and distribution centre for used clothing available to needy persons for the taking.

The accused on coming to Chatham expanded the existing social and recreational programme carried on at the church. With the approval of a responsible church committee, he organized a senior young people's group, a Tuxis group for boys in their late teens, a Sigma-C group for boys in their early teens and, subsequently, a teen-town and youth anonymous programme. This last-mentioned group was designed to attract to the church young persons who had no traditional attachment and to provide them with an opportunity to discuss personal problems on a confidential group basis. The result of this expanded programme was to keep the church buildings in constant use by a range of young people. The accused set aside, in addition, a counselling period from 4.30 to 6 p.m. for teen-age persons and this was made known through church publications. There is evidence that many youngsters visited the accused in his office for general talk and that he made himself available to them, even lending them small amounts of money, apparently in line with a social conception of his ministry.

The young people named in the charges brought against the accused admittedly engaged in delinquent conduct in the church premises. Neither the church nor the accused can be held responsible for this simply because they permitted access to the church unless they were, or should have been, aware of what was happening and allowed it to continue. There was evidence that the frequent dances held in the church were chaperoned, there was a janitor who serviced the church premises, and the accused's secretary was there from 10 a.m. to 5 p.m. or later. What is alleged against the accused are not acts of omission but of commission, and, as already indicated, of the 24 acts specified in eight counts, nine were brought home to him under five counts.

Varied grounds of appeal were submitted on behalf of the appellant, but it is only necessary for me to deal with one of them; namely, that the learned trial Judge failed to apply the rule of caution as to the danger of conviction on the uncorroborated evidence of accomplices.

The learned trial Judge gave detailed reasons for his judgment. He did not consider the matter of the evidence of accomplices at all. . . .

It is now a settled law that in a criminal trial, where a person who is an accomplice gives evidence on behalf of a prosecution, it is the duty of the Judge to warn the jury that, although they may convict upon his evidence, it is dangerous to do so unless it is corroborated. . . .

The reasons of the learned trial Judge make it clear that he did not consider it necessary, as a matter of law, to pay heed to that warning in weighing the evidence. If the evidence against the accused did consist of the evidence of accomplices, then there was an error in law. . . .

In the circumstances of this case, in my opinion they were accomplices. . . .

In my opinion, there was an error in law in the failure by the learned trial Judge, when weighing the evidence, to take account of his duty to assess the evidence of the participants in the sexual acts as being that of accomplices and not of independent witnesses.

This conclusion makes it unnecessary to deal with the ground of appeal based upon the refusal by the Court of Appeal to consider the self-contradictory evidence of two witnesses who testified at the trial. I would, however, like to express my view that the fact that the witnesses in question had testified at the trial on the issues on which further examination was sought, and had been subject at trial to cross-examination, is not a valid ground for the refusal to hear such evidence.

In my opinion, the appeal should be allowed and a new trial directed.

The dissenting judgment given by Mr. J. Ritchie argued that the juveniles were not accomplices and therefore corroboration was unnecessary:

It appears to me to be clear that the danger to be guarded against in cases of sexual offences is that the complainant, through a motive of spite, vengeance, hysteria or perhaps gain by way of blackmail, may make false accusations against which the accused, by reason of the nature of the charges, has no means of defence except his own unsupported denial. It is the fact of sexual misconduct that requires corroboration and this rule of practice can have no application to a case like the present in which such conduct is freely admitted by the persons concerned. I am satisfied that there is no error in law in the judge failing to mention this rule in his reasons for judgment.

He argues that the juveniles were not accomplices in that they did not participate in the "acts of contributing" but rather committed acts of sexual immorality as a result.

The fact that the appellant's "contribution" to their delinquency resulted in some of the child witnesses having sexual intercourse does not, in my opinion, make them accessories after the fact to the offence of making the "contribution" with which the appellant is charged. It follows, in my view, that in order to have been accomplices . . . the child witnesses would have had to be *participes criminis* in and therefore subject to prosecution for, the offence of contributing to the delinquencies of the children named in the charges against the appellant or contributing to some other delinquencies concerning which they had testified as to his guilt to which they had been parties.

In a rarely seen separate judgment, Mr. Justice Wishart Spence agreed with Mr. Justice Markland and then added strength to his statement by presenting several additional points:

These five children (Crown witnesses) particularly as well as other witnesses were all juveniles who had on their own repeated admissions been guilty of the most serious sexual misconduct. It was the whole import of their evidence that they had been encouraged or even led into that conduct by the words and acts of the accused. It would be natural that children making such confessions of their own misconduct would be only too anxious to seek excuse in attempting to put, whether it be to foist or not, the blame on the adult accused. To consider their evidence as that of competent adult witnesses under the circumstances, in my opinion, constituted the gravest error. Their testimony should have been weighed in the light of these most serious circumstances. With respect, I am of the opinion that the learned trial Judge did not do so. Having noted the inconsistencies of their evidence, and having shown he was fully aware of their equivocal position, he nevertheless proceeded to assign credibility to their testimony, it would appear, basing such view upon their demeanour and not keeping in mind their history.

Findings of facts are, of course, for the learned trial Judge but such findings must be made upon a consideration of the proper factors. I am of the opinion that the learned trial Judge here, in the sentence I have quoted, deprived himself of one of the proper factors and proceeded, in his assignment of the credibility of the witnesses, to exhibit that he had so deprived himself.

I am of the opinion that the learned trial Judge erred in his assessing the credibility of the witnesses not only by failing to view with sufficient caution the evidence of children given in the circumstances to which I have referred but by failing to consider the evidence given by the accused in denial of such evidence of the children with any proper appreciation of the character of the accused who gave such evidence. There was adduced at trial for the defence not only the evidence of the accused but, *inter alia,* evidence testifying to the good character of the accused . . .

Without giving in detail the evidence of these twelve character witnesses, suffice it to say they gave very strong character evidence in favour of the accused man. The learned trial Judge, although he realized and acknowledged that the accused was a clergyman and had been so for years, did not, in weighing the evidence of the many child witnesses for the prosecution whose admitted conduct may well be characterized as disreputable, assess that evidence having in view the denial of it by the accused whose character was vouched for by the very large volume of evidence to which I have referred.

The learned trial Judge did not refer at all to the character evidence in giving his reasons. . . . I am of the opinion that the accused on whose behalf that evidence had been adduced was entitled to have that evidence of his character cited and considered by the trial Judge in arriving at his decision.

I find it interesting to read again the summation that my lawyer, C. E. Perkins, presented to Judge Fox at the conclusion of the first trial and to note how the Supreme Court judgment, and that of Mr. Bora Laskin, bear out almost to the letter the lawyer's argument.

Mr. Perkins had contended that credibility was the major issue in the case and warned the judge of the danger of convicting on uncorroborated evidence of juveniles. Judge Fox did not accept his argument; the Supreme Court did. Mr. Perkins had carefully listed the discrepancies in the Crown witnesses' testimony in order to prove their unreliability. Judge Fox ignored this; in fact, he believed their stories in spite of the contradictions. Mr. Justice Laskin and the Supreme Court Justices sided with Mr. Perkins.

Mr. Perkins called the Crown witnesses "promiscuous, prevaricating, incorrigible sneaks". "It is almost impossible to list the discrepancies in the evidence of Crown witnesses; they contradict themselves and each other at every turn. These are not normal differences expected when witnesses are telling the truth."

Referring to one specific event involving three witnesses, Mr. Perkins describes the evidence as "so confusing, so contradictory that it is a tangled skein of comments not only impossible to unravel but impossible to believe. In very brief terms, it is such a mess it can't be separated and I submit is not worthy of an attempt at separation."

Mr. Perkins contrasted these Crown witnesses with those of the Defence. "These Defence witnesses bore a marked decency and integrity. They told a different story. They said that Mr. Horsburgh had helped them with their school problems, counselled them when they had problems and was a friend to them."

Mr. Perkins blamed the Chatham Police Department for encouraging the Crown witnesses to expand a story that was false in the first place.

Said Mr. Perkins, "The failure of the Chatham Police to question either Mr. Horsburgh or the chaperones who worked at the dances may have had a great bearing on the degree of anger or 'what have you' that started the matter. If these teenagers made up this story and nothing came up to counteract it, then this story could start to roll and expand."

"When the whole picture is laid out and the conduct of most of the young people around the church and the rooms available to them are known, we have a situation which is consistent only with the attitude of a high-minded Christian cleric who has in his mind that the majority of teen-agers today are decent people. He does not anticipate that a small group will use their degeneracy to attack."

Mr. Dubin, in the Appeal courts, followed essentially the

same line of reasoning. Again, the matter of credibility was the main issue. He contended that it was highly unlikely that an ordained minister called to serve God, a man of letters, graduate of several universities and fourteen years in the ministry would suddenly become an instrument of the devil and engage in planned debauchery. "Who are we to believe?" asked Mr. Dubin, "The damning evidence of teen-agers of unsavory and loose character – themselves guilty of sexual acts, or Mr. Horsburgh and his parade of character witnesses who gave evidence of his good reputation in the community?"

Mr. Dubin listed the Crown witnesses and their crimes that didn't affect their credibility in the eyes of the judge and then went on to say that respectable defence witnesses had been discredited completely by the judge.

"There had been thirty defence witnesses, including twelve character witnesses, although you'd never know it from the judgment," he said.

Mr. Dubin accused the judge of using a double standard when assessing the credibility of Crown and Defence witnesses. "It appeared that unless the judge could find a motive for Crown witnesses lying on the stand, he accepted their evidence."

When I read the Supreme Court judgment, I am reminded also of a statement I released to the press the day after I was arrested. It read as follows:

While it is not pleasant to be accused, it gives me a chance to defend myself and explain my attempt to lift these children up and make them law-abiding citizens. If the authorities believe that I was contributing to their delinquency, I feel my interest in them will be vindicated when the evidence is known.

Far from encouraging any improper activity by them, I and the adults working with me were doing all in our power to convince these young people that the pattern of conduct that they exhibited before joining Youth Anonymous was in error and we didn't have any expectation of an overnight change in their attitudes.

I am entirely innocent of the charges and I intend to attempt to make this abundantly clear when the time to do so arrives.

Another person who was vindicated by the Supreme Court judgment was the Reverend Ronald Smeaton, author of *The Horsburgh Affair*. The book was published in 1966 between the original trial and the first appeal. It was reviewed by over 300 periodicals and newspapers in Canada, most of which I had the opportunity to read. In all, I came across only one unfavorable report; it was damning. This one appeared in *The United Church Observer*. Its thesis can be summed up in five words taken from the review: "The book is a failure." The reviewer attacked Smeaton's literary style and not the argument of the book – as if the former were the main issue. The publisher was also personally attacked. He saw fit to publish 30,000 copies of the book; therefore, his major concern must have been to make money! The review just didn't make sense. The book was far from a failure. Not only did it have a good sale and a wide reading, but it brought me support from far and wide. A reading of this book is almost tantamount to a reading of the Supreme Court judgment. Smeaton treated, in depth, the issues of corroboration and credibility, and carefully documented his findings. In a concise and vivid style, he describes the extenuating circumstances of the trial. In my opinion, the book is a masterpiece and gives an even clearer picture of the whole issue than the trial transcript itself.

At this point, three years after I was first declared a guilty man, I was once more innocent. Even though I was to be charged once again, and once again brought before a Juvenile Court in Chatham under these charges, I was never again to be convicted.

CHAPTER 13

The Crown's second attack on me in the retrial ordered by the Supreme Court was hamstrung. The prosecuting attorney could no longer get the co-operation of those witnesses who had been previously vulnerable to him. Even those who were still willing to co-operate were now invalidated by the evidence from the affidavits and by the willingness of other former Crown witnesses to reverse their original statements. Also, underlying the comments of the Supreme Court judgment was an implicit rejection of the procedures employed by the Crown Attorney in his courtroom behavior with the witnesses.

By this time, I was anxious, almost desperate, to complete the legal procedures and to reshape my life as an innocent man. The Crown, on the other hand, seemed strangely anxious to prolong the preliminaries and to avoid the final retrial.

On three different occasions, the date for the retrial was set and then delayed. When asked the reason behind this, the Crown Attorney's Department claimed they were having difficulties locating the Crown witnesses.

Originally, fourteen people gave evidence that contributed to my conviction. Eight charges were brought in, and I was found guilty on five of them. This time, only three of these witnesses were available, according to the Crown, and their evidence was to be amalgamated into one charge. Apparently, the police and the Attorney General's Office were incapable of finding the other eleven witnesses.

We found all fourteen witnesses. Instead of being unavailable, they were no longer willing to give the same stories. We discovered that most, if not all of them, had been located by the Crown, had been questioned, and eventually were issued subpoenas. Of the fourteen, three were used; the other eleven had become unco-operative.

Between June, 1967 and early in the New Year of 1968, delays and postponements were continually occurring. The Ontario Government called an election in September. The Progressive Conservative party returned a full slate of Members to the Government from the Chatham area. On the next occasion when the date for the retrial was set, all proceedings went ahead as planned.

Under Mr. Justice J. H. Kirkpatrick, a newly appointed Crown Attorney introduced one charge, which involved only three of the original witnesses. Their testimony was heard within the space of a single morning. That afternoon, both the Crown and the Defence concluded their cases. The Defence stated simply that the Crown's case had fallen apart and that the accused was not confronted with anything that he had to deny. The Crown Attorney agreed, and entered a submission of complicity with the Defence.

The key witness in the case was a boy whom Judge Fox had described as "intelligent, frank and honest . . . I accept his evidence in its entirety". At the retrial, the boy admitted to Mr. Dubin in cross-examination that he had been before the courts for incorrigibility before the first trial and that during the first trial he made an appearance at another court charged with stealing a car radio, was convicted of the offense, and put on probation. Mr. Justice Kirkpatrick, at the retrial, said he was not impressed with this boy's testimony.

In his judgment, Justice Kirkpatrick said: "Whether time has eroded memories or reflection has improved them, we don't know"; but the evidence before him was so unrelated to the charges and so vague that I had to be acquitted. He stressed that he was dealing only with the charges and evidence before him and was making no comment on other charges, other witnesses, other trials or the process by which "there was so lightly taken away a man's professional reputation. None of those arose in this hearing." Justice Kirkpatrick declared that there was no evidence of contributing to juvenile delinquency and found that I was not guilty. By three o'clock I was once again legally a free and innocent man.

Since the trials, many people have asked me what basically led to my conviction on such obvious flimsy charges. Why did it happen at all? Who was responsible? The answer may lie not in the specific orders of any one person but in the spontaneous actions of many. When the establishment closes its ranks, when authority takes arms against what it mistakenly believes to be corruption, there is no need for the posting of specific battalion orders. Within the hierarchy, each member knows what is required of him, what he must do. During the investigation and trial, each man did it. The proceedings against me had a certain inevitability. Once put into motion, they gained a relentless momentum of their own which it subsequently became impossible to stop.

CHAPTER 14

I have received no official communication from Park Street United Church since the crisis befell me in 1964. They did not even acknowledge my resignation; they have never sent as much as a note or card offering the crumbs. When I won my retrial, again they were conspicuous by their silence. I heard from countless other congregations through their Sessions. Individuals in Park Street Church contacted me; but there was nothing official. There is, of course, an obvious reason for this: the old guard still has the upper hand in the conduct of church affairs and still insists on preserving the status quo.

I was to see my friends and supporters in the church utterly bewildered, longing for a happy fellowship but finding only disillusion. These people were the best support any minister could have, devoted to a large-spirited inclusive Christianity. Amid the tumult, they did their best to build a church that was vigorously active in its work, believing the best attack was not recrimination but a practical illustration of what a church could mean in a city such as Chatham. They realized that such a struggle in a congregation could not be tolerated indefinitely. So rightly or wrongly, when it became plain that the rebellious minority had achieved its purpose and was once again in power, many of these devoted workers, wearying of the fight and unwilling themselves to function as a contentious minority, withdrew from the church and for sometime struggled to found a new congregation. These efforts were thwarted by Kent Presbytery and finally, they either drifted from the church altogether or went to other congregations.

Early in June, 1965, I resigned from the ministry of the United Church of Canada. My legal expenses were mounting and I could think of only one source of funds – my pension contributions of seventeen years and more. In order to collect it, I had to resign. I had asked the Church through both its Moderator and Department of Pensions for a loan or a grant. One assured me that such was available; but the other was just as certain that it was not. Finally, I received a letter from Dr. George Tuttle, Secretary of Pensions, informing me that no help could be given and that there was no compassionate fund for ministers in need.

My main reason for leaving the church was the lack of support, the continuing gossip that I encountered in church circles wherever I went, and, most disappointing of all, the lack of even so much as compassion from the Body of Christ.

After my resignation, which seemed to lift a heavy burden from my shoulders, I had the feeling that the trouble would still follow me. I found it hard to believe that a church that had obviously already condemned me and found me guilty would likely change. I felt somewhat like the convict who escapes from the security of a life sentence in a penitentiary, who knows the police are after him yet must build a new life anyway. I felt somewhat like the Jews in the days of Nehemiah as they faced the Arabians, the Amonites, and the Ashdodites.

They which builded the wall, and they that bare burdens, with those that laded, everyone with one of his hands wrought in the work, and with the other hand held a weapon. For the builders, everyone had his sword girded by his side.

I anticipated neither understanding nor tangible help from the Kent Presbytery of which I had been a member and which was most responsible for me, and I was not mistaken. The London Conference of the United Church reacted to my resignation more with hostility than indifference. Damning rumors still flew, prejudice and intolerance continued to rear their ugly heads. It is revealing, however, that those people who worked closely with me over the years are still militantly in the ranks of my supporters and unhesitatingly call upon my ministry when I can be of help.

Twelve Chatham businessmen started a fund to appeal the original conviction and to assist with my living expenses. What I would have done without this help I do not know, because I had been without salary for most of a year. These men filled the gap left by Presbytery's reluctance to take up the cudgels for me and even now they send me the occasional cheque. At least, they never fail to inquire about my welfare.

A year after my conviction, the United Church's Board of Evangelism and Social Service decided that something should be done. After months of deliberation, a grant of $5,000 was set aside for my living expenses and was given to me as I needed it. This money resulted from the efforts of the late Reverend J. Ray Hord, Board secretary, and here I pay tribute to him for his intervention on my behalf. This gesture seemed to be an answer to prayer, for I was destitute at the time.

In August, 1966, a time when funds were again in particularly short supply, I found a job with a Toronto travel agency. This was, in effect, my first secular employment since leaving the ministry and the adjustment was not made easily. However, my employers were kind, understood my situation and, with a mixture of forbearance on both sides, we got along amicably. Understandably, some of my fellow employees were not completely familiar with the facts of the Chatham incidents; but the initial uneasiness that was occasionally evident in the office soon passed and it was not long before my colleagues aligned themselves with my cause in a solid show of support.

My foremost advocate within the company was its general manager, Miss Helen Craven, an efficient, cheerful person who, on learning that several thousand dollars were still needed for my appeal before the Supreme Court of Canada, promptly organized a drive for funds. Joined by businessmen and other professional groups, the campaign brought in most of the money needed at that time. I shall never forget the day when two dozen of Miss Craven's staff turned up at the office to type and stuff the appeal envelopes. Or the several kind employees who, in the weeks that followed, devoted their lunch hours to making out receipts for donations. Of course, Miss Craven met with opposition from some quarters. Nasty anonymous letters came in; but in her magnanimity, she ignored them. If, in fact, a letter was not signed she would refuse to read it. The fund reached the required $5,000, and even after the Supreme Court hearing money still came in.

Unfortunately, this spirit of understanding and help was not manifest in other quarters. About this time, late in 1966, the General Council of the United Church of Canada was meeting in Waterloo, and from the Bay of Quinte Conference came a memorial that called for "love, compassion, and concern for Rev. Russell D. Horsburgh". The motion read as follows:

Whereas it is the essence of the Gospel that we love and manifest active concern for our fellows, whether clerical or lay;

And whereas the Rev. Russell David Horsburgh, formerly minister of Park Street United Church in Chatham, Ontario, is in dire need of that love and concern;

And whereas the Board of Evangelism and Social Service of the United Church of Canada has authorized a compassionate grant of up to $5,000 to be expended on Russell Horsburgh's behalf, and the general public is of the opinion that he has received such assistance;

And whereas the said Russell Horsburgh, as of this date, in nearly two years of misfortunate circumstances has received only $800 and one perfunctory visit from our Church's national offices;

Therefore be it resolved that the General Council be petitioned to take immediate action, through proper channels, to evince substantial and concrete concern and love for the Rev. Russell David Horsburgh, a former United Church cleric who left the United Church ministry voluntarily, and in good standing insofar as the courts of the church are concerned.

Harmless in word and intent, its purpose could not have been anything but beneficial. Certainly, it was not in any way an affront even to those clergy who, in the face of impressive new evidence to the contrary that was prevalent at the time, insisted on believing only the worst about me. Nevertheless, the memorial was denounced even before it reached the floor of the general session and, when it finally came to a vote, was soundly rejected. My feelings at that time defy description. I wrote at once to the Council secretary:

I have read with disappointment the majority decision of General Council with respect to the Memorial brought forward, on my behalf, by the Bay of Quinte Conference.

Notwithstanding the results, which are most discouraging and disheartening in my time of trouble, I feel it incumbant upon me to thank the Council for considering my problem, and particularly those whose sense of Christian charity caused them to support the Memorial.

It is regrettable that inaccuracies were found in the Memorial. The form of the Memorial, which I read, was accurate as far as I could see, and I am sure that any inaccuracies must have been very minor in nature.

I shall have to continue to use my own resources, whatever they may prove to be, to pursue alone the seemingly difficult and endless road to justice. I already owe in excess of $10,000.00 and will have to be responsible for several thousands more to finance my appeal to the Supreme Court of Canada.

Again, I assure you of my innocence and I pray that no other clergyman will ever have to tread this path.

Would you please convey to General Council my gratitude and ask for their prayers on my behalf.

I was to receive no reply and I am given to understand that my letter was not even announced let alone read to the general assembly.

My feelings were reflected further in this writer's letter

which appeared in the *London Free Press* addressed to the General Council:

SIR:

This is addressed to Rev. J. A. Davidson, General Council of the United Church. The appalling hypocrisy that characterizes the church today was never better exemplified than by your denunciation last Friday of a simple motion at the general session of the General Council of the United Church calling for "love, compassion and concern for the Rev. R. D. Horsburgh."

If this motion was not an expression of the essence of simple Christianity to an afflicted human being, then what on earth was it? Yet you, a minister, dared stand and speak against it: you, who in all your professed words and works are, of all men, supposed to stand for brotherly love to all, the good and the bad, the socially acceptable and the damned.

Your action on Friday strikes at the core of brotherhood and well testifies to all that is amiss with the shell of hypocrisy that is the church today.

I hope – how I hope – that the report of Friday's session was in error. But if it was not then there is no hope at all – for the confused and bewildered, for the lost among us, for the church. To reject this motion was shameful, arrogant contempt of God more than anyone else.

Union with the Anglicans? Far better, surely, to unite with the people first: the crisp-suited acceptable and the shuffling sorry outcasts.

London S. F. S.

Subsequently, the Reverend J. A. Davidson, the minister who had moved rejection of the Memorial, wrote to me explaining that he had opposed it because of what he called its "overly-emotional tones". His letter failed to convince and I was left with the impression that the United Church of Canada was more interested in keeping itself free from any taint of disrepute by association than in offering "love, compassion, and concern" to an afflicted brother minister who had served its cause for nearly 20 years.

In May, 1968, four months after I was cleared by the retrial, I was given the remainder of the $5,000 grant set aside by the Board of Evangelism and Social Service of the United Church of Canada. Dr. Ray Hord had passed away suddenly early in the year. His post at the Church's head office was taken temporarily by Dr. James R. Mutchmor whose signature appeared on the cheque that I received. Along with that final payment of the grant came a revealing letter from which the following is taken:

I think this is the time to make a clear statement about the relationship between yourself and this Board, including the definite word that this Board will not consider anything further in the way of a compassionate grant to you or a supporting grant for any work you may undertake. I think you will realize there is nothing personal in this statement. It is the kind of definite word which we would put in a letter in concluding any other agreement.

When I was finally cleared by the courts, a host of friends (and strangers, too) began to encourage me to return to the ministry. I expected that the church might take the initiative and restore me. But it obviously was not going to be automatic; indeed, almost a year after the acquittal I was still waiting to hear some official word from the church. So, in the fall of 1968, I applied for re-admission.

The application had to be made before Kent Presbytery, which had jurisdiction over Chatham. I could see little hope of success in this area; its members had previously shown strong prejudice against me. I was called before the Presbytery executive and began to plead my case. It was not long before I knew which way my application was going.

"Many people at Park Street Church will leave if you return to the ministry," was almost the first remark made, and it was spoken sourly by that church's present minister. "Don't you think you should consider the good of the church and not go back?" It was more a decision than a suggestion.

I began to argue against this line of thinking; but he was already speaking on another. "You were not very strenuously prosecuted at the retrial," he said.

There was some kind of insinuation behind his words; but its significance escaped me. I merely replied that the obvious reason for the lack of a strenuous prosecution was the lack of any evidence with which to prosecute.

But it was hopeless. They were dead set against me in the majority, reminding me of the consequences of "stirring things up again" and how I refused their offers of help in the past. Offers of help? I recall nothing in the way of an offer of help from any of them! In the end, thirty voted against me, ten for. I asked them to reconsider, but they refused. Their minds were made up: I was out, and that was that. This, then, is Christianity in the eyes of Kent Presbytery. The courts had ruled me innocent of wrongdoing; but not the so-called advocates of that gentle man who had walked the earth 2,000 years ago. The price of His "crime" was nails in flesh and wood; mine was nails of scorn and a devastated respectability.

Early in 1965 I had wandered into a church in Toronto where a visiting minister was conducting protracted services. I cannot quite explain why I felt led to attend that service; I had not been accustomed to going to strange churches. I heard singing from the nearby street and it was beautiful. This, I think, and some act of divine providence drew me to that place. That afternoon I was to hear the deeply stirring songs of the recording artists, Ron and Sharon Price. It was singing that obviously came from the fullness of young lives dedicated to a spirit-filled ministry. The sermon, too, was just as moving and it came at a time when my spirits were low. I wrote to the young minister and thanked him for his help. This sparked the beginning of a friendship with Reverend Ron and Sharon Price that has done more to buoy me up in the Christian faith than many experiences I've had along the way. They took me not only into their hearts but into their home. When my case came before the Supreme Court of Canada, these young people prayed fervently for me both privately and within their congregations. They organized a Prayer Chain that extended across the country so that my friends everywhere were joined together in this communion, taking time each day to bear me up before the throne of Grace. One can never forget such sacrificial kindness.

My joy knew no bounds when Ron and Sharon Price agreed one day to help re-establish me in the ministry by co-founding with me the "Church in the Streets" in Toronto, and its major project, "Youth Anonymous". For over a year now, we've worked hand in hand building a movement that we hope will be worthy of recognition as one of the most relevant church witnesses found anywhere today. We've travelled together on the "Up With Youth" Crusade to almost one hundred centres in Ontario and Quebec, and we have invitations from every part of Canada. Young, earnest, and vigorous, Ron Price is making the "Church in the Streets" a vital force in Toronto. His ministry is primarily with youth. He finds them in police courts and jails, seeks out their haunts on the streets, counsels those in trouble and directs them to agencies where they can be helped. He organizes them into Youth Anonymous links, establishes big-brother, big-sister relationships, encourages them to return to school and assists them in finding jobs. His sheer power of personality and clear grit have made him the effective minister to youth that he is. I never cease to remind myself how fortunate I am to be associated in the ministry with this fine young couple who seem to possess all the graces of Christian character.

CHAPTER 15

As I look back over these momentous years, I admit to few regrets – except, perhaps, at my own shortcomings and mistakes. Most people who came within my sphere were kind; countless friendships were forged and nourished. Churches prospered under my ministry and, were I to do it again, I would once more stand for a radical religion – a religion as modern as the twentieth century and so relevant as to inbue these troubled times with shining new hope and purpose, a throbbing vitality without which the church is a shell.

I believe the world is impatient for such a faith. If it is to come, however, the ministry must lead the way in breaking the fetters of the past. Ministers must not fear being misunderstood, misrepresented, persecuted, even crucified. If they believe in a resurrection, their agonies will not be a burden.

Most importantly, the persecution must not be met with bitterness. As the late Albert Schweitzer once put it:

> I must be ready to forgive lies directed against me because so many times my own conduct has been blotted by lies. I must forgive the lovelessness, the hatred, the slander, the fraud, the arrogance which I encounter, since I myself have so often lacked love . . . and I must forgive without noise and fuss. In general, I do not succeed in forgiving fully; I do not get as far as being always just. But he who

tries to live by this principle, simple and hard as it is, will know the real adventures and triumphs of the soul.

With such a spirit, our pains and failures can be stepping-stones to higher achievements. There can, as well, be real happiness when it is not sought after but is incidental to the great tasks and goals we strive to reach.

I know what it is to be stripped naked of reputation and career, smeared by the fiercely indecent attacks of small-minded, vindictive people who know as little about the tenets of their religion as the dumb beasts whose braying they imitate. There have been moments – bleak, black, frustrating moments – when, like Job, I was tempted to curse God and to die. I know what it is to be a wanderer on the face of the earth, a tramp taking the handouts that I needed to keep alive from day to day, strained to the uttermost of financial and spiritual need. But I am determined to win in spite of all.

I want my experience to prove that a minister can overcome his fears and survive the most vicious attacks. I want it to prove that most people believe in freedom of thought, speech, and religion and will rally to a man who exercises that right. No one in trouble and seeming disgrace need seek the anonymity of faraway fields. He needs only a clear conscience, the courage of his convictions, a willingness to work, confidence in his fellowmen, and faith in God. With these he can face the future unafraid. As Paracelsus said, in Robert Browning's phrase:

If I stoop
Into a tremendous sea of cloud,
It is but for a time; I press God's lamp
Close to my breast; it's splendour soon or late,
Will pierce the gloom. I shall emerge one day.

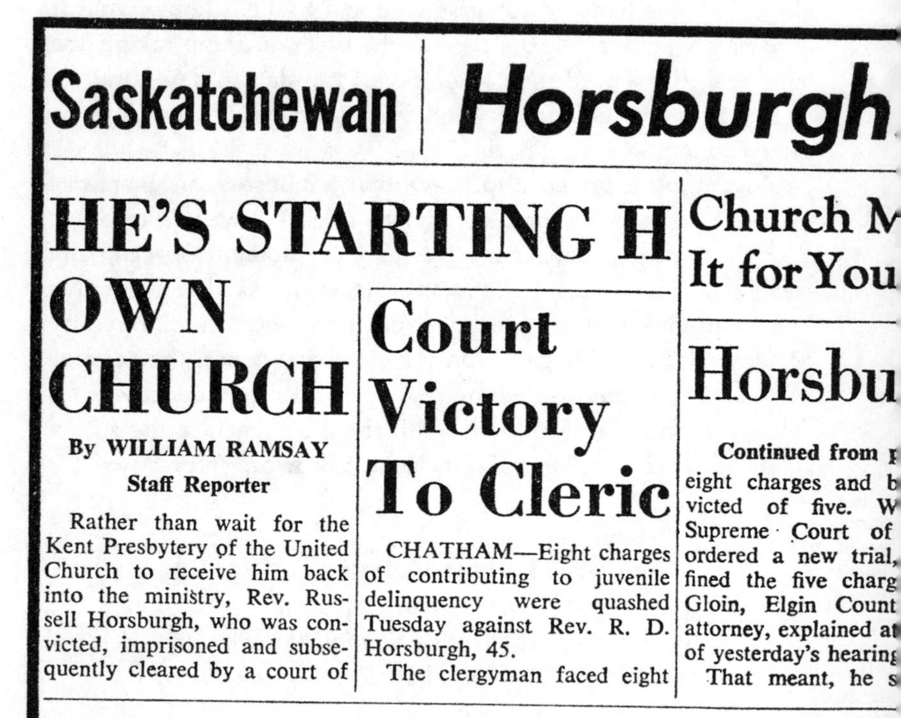

Saskatchewan | Horsburgh

HE'S STARTING HIS OWN CHURCH

By WILLIAM RAMSAY
Staff Reporter

Rather than wait for the Kent Presbytery of the United Church to receive him back into the ministry, Rev. Russell Horsburgh, who was convicted, imprisoned and subsequently cleared by a court of

Court Victory To Cleric

CHATHAM—Eight charges of contributing to juvenile delinquency were quashed Tuesday against Rev. R. D. Horsburgh, 45.

The clergyman faced eight

Church M
It for You

Horsbu

Continued from p
eight charges and b
victed of five. W
Supreme Court of
ordered a new trial,
fined the five charg
Gloin, Elgin Count
attorney, explained a
of yesterday's hearing
That meant, he s

Horsburgh penniless but rec

PART 3
WHERE DO I GO FROM HERE?

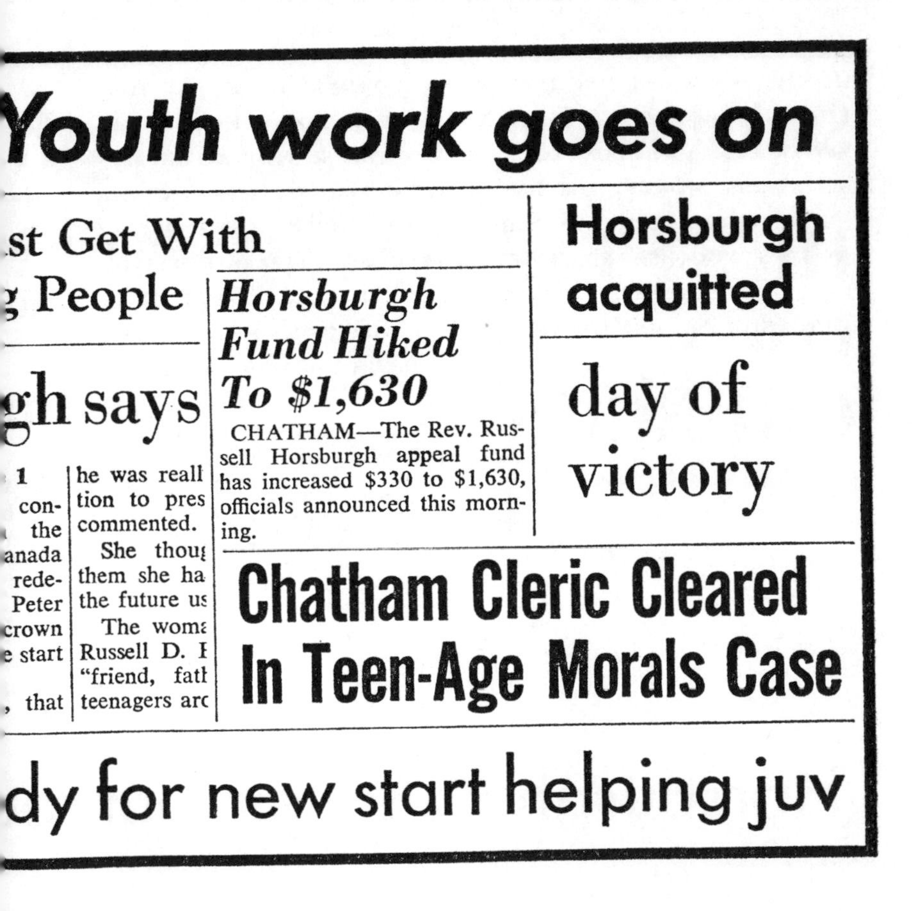

Youth work goes on

st Get With
g People

gh says

1 con- the anada rede- Peter crown e start , that

he was reall tion to pres commented.
She thou them she ha the future us
The woma Russell D. I "friend, fatl teenagers arc

Horsburgh Fund Hiked To $1,630

CHATHAM—The Rev. Russell Horsburgh appeal fund has increased $330 to $1,630, officials announced this morning.

Horsburgh acquitted

day of victory

Chatham Cleric Cleared In Teen-Age Morals Case

dy for new start helping juv

THE NEW ERA IS USHERING ITSELF IN BY A NEW RELIGION, AND THAT RELIGION IS NOT MERELY THE CHRISTIAN RELIGION, BUT AN EXPANSION OF IT. . . . RELIGION NOW BECOMES THE SUM OF ALL HUMAN ASPIRATIONS; WORSHIP THE SUM OF ALL HUMAN SERVICES; AND ALL THE WORKERS ARE THE WORSHIPPERS. THE CHURCH LOSES ONE BY ONE ITS FUNCTIONS, AND CEASES TO EXIST AS A SEPARATE INSTITUTION . . . BUT ITS PLACE IS TAKEN BY THE UNIVERSAL COMMUNION OF A HUMANITY PRESSING FORWARD TO THE PRIZE OF ITS HIGH CALLING.

HENRY DEMAREST LLOYD

CHAPTER 16

The question most frequently put to me is: "What will you do now?" Behind the question there is no doubt the unspoken assumption that whatever lies ahead for me, it is not in the ministry. But this is wrong. For wherever I do go from here – it will assuredly be within some form of ministry. In spite of the fires through which I have gone, I still regard the ministry as the greatest challenge to which any man or woman can be called. If a minister forsook his calling at the time when it demanded most from him he would be betraying his very integrity as a person. For one enters the ministry expecting that there will be crisis, failure, and frustration. At the moment, that crisis and frustration is at a peak; but I am encouraged by the plain fact that so far in my life there has been a balance of failure and success. Let it be clear then. A minister I have been. A minister I shall remain.

But fires burn that which passes through them, changing, reshaping, and re-coloring. The Chatham ordeal – and the many events and principles of my ministry that went before – has served to burn away at my early attitudes and expectations toward the ministry. It was a low fire for years, reaching the melting point only in Chatham. I have learned much from the experience, and the ministry that I envisage for myself *now* is drastically different from what it was even five years ago.

The most immediate difference is a personal one – and this is true of the great watershed experiences that men have had. New platforms result when there is a new person. And the new platform that will characterize my future ministry will depend very much on some new personal approaches. In my case there are two very personal changes.

First, a besetting sin of many would-be reformers is their impatience with the people who stand by the "old ways". Anyone who sets out to change the fundamental patterns of human behavior had better face the fact that it is going to take a long time. Even to change one's own character takes years. Human character or institutions do not change rapidly or much. To have changed them even a little is a solid accomplishment. One can learn a lesson from a simple demonstration in physics. If an object moving in a straight line is deflected even a little it will end up at a great distance from where it otherwise would have been. If a human life or human institution is deflected on its course just a little, the eventual result could be astounding. Any minister who wishes to be also a reformer must bear this in mind. Few reforms on a grand scale are begun and finished within one lifetime. And no amount of pulpit barking will both sow seeds of discontent with present ways and reap a harvest of radically changed lives or institutions.

My ministry in the future will therefore be more gracious, more ready to accept with some degree of humor the foibles of men. This will not mean an abandonment of complete honesty in human relations. Always there will have to be straight talk. I shall never hold back my opinions for fear of offending someone. But with this I shall have to realize that we are all human, that all of us find it hard to change those parts of our life that represent all we have ever stood for.

This is true for all reform; but in my case it is clearest in church reform. When a minister arrives in a situation that personally enrages his scale of values, he is tempted to clean house with a fast broom. Only instead of one broom it is usually ten brooms that he tries to wield all at once and in ten rooms! This he often does in total disregard of those people who have developed and stood by the very programs that disappoint him. The result is that great clouds of dust are raised, feelings are hurt, human personality is ignored in the cause of "reform," and in the end the minister finds himself standing alone in the midst of a pile of debris. He may have "made his point"; but there is nothing to show for it. And instead of being able to implement positive programs in place of the old, each of the areas of concern is in a state of confusion as bad as it was before.

After being able to stand back and look at my ministry for the past two years, any "reform programs" that I institute in the future will be in concentrated areas. I shall take one problem at a time, work with it long enough to know all possible sides of it, persuade a small core of people to see the need for change, and then try to see it through to completion. With one project firmly established, energy can be turned to another. The result of such a method should be that the minister will be not so much a "lone crusader" (though this may often be necessary) as one working with a group of concerned people to correct a wrong state of affairs.

The second thing I have learned is the error of an "I'm right, you're wrong" attitude. A minister is constantly encouraged by his worst self to believe that every idea he has is angelic, while the ideas he is trying to displace are diabolic. Perhaps it is the superstition of some kind of priestly purity that has rooted itself in the subconscious of many well-intentioned clergymen. His reforms are supported by a "holier-than-thou" sense of superiority – a kind of modern-day Divine Right. He easily expresses a feeling that the laymen of the church he serves are involved in sin to a degree to which he could not possibly be involved. As a matter of fact, he too quickly dismisses the fact that all men are involved in the contemporary sin of exaggerated materialism – and that he, as well as they – profit by it. There is no aspect of social sin today in which the minister is not involved as much as his people. When we think of struggling with the conformist patterns that have become so much a part of our lives, we have to think of struggling with them together. It must not be a matter of *my* telling *you* what *you* have to do about them. Whatever is done about them must be done together, and with the common burden of being responsible for them.

But when one has taken stock of himself before going into action, the time comes for definite planning for the way in which he will act. The two examples of ways in which my personal point of view has been altered are only illustrations of many other insights that I have gained. It is time now to state some of the planks of the platform that will certainly characterize my future ministry.

Perhaps every minister should have an opportunity to stand outside the active life of the church after a long time of being involved with it. After having worked within the structure of the church for almost twenty years I could see with clarity some things I had not noticed enough before. Each of the things that I see now as being urgent problems for the church is something on which I have preached or thought about many times. But the buzz of activity that surrounds the minister makes it impossible for him to push his thinking to a concrete plan of action. Church work often causes an inertia in the matters of real importance.

Hence, my present cry is for a church outside the church. The church as it exists is absolutely incapable of being a twentieth-century reality for the majority of men who live in our age. Furthermore, this fact is true because of two assumptions about the church that most ministers and laymen accept without question – two assumptions that are twins because they are similar in their basic meaning. They are two carry-overs from previous ways of thinking about life and organizing life, and have no place whatever in our age. They are the scourges of DOGMA and DENOMINATIONALISM. They are twins because dogma needs the support of denomination, and a denomination needs the support of a dogma. And because the church leans so heavily on both these assumptions, a church that is stripped of them (a church for our age) will be completely different from the church most of us know. It will be a church outside the church.

We have been abundantly assured that the church is identified with ideas and practices in which the modern man has not the slightest interest. Not only does he not interest himself in the things that concern the church, he does not believe in them. He has simply moved out of the world in which the denominational churches were born (both Protestant and Roman Catholic – for the latter is just as much denominational as the former) and still live. What the church is thinking and saying he does not know, or if he knows, he does not care.

The creeds are the obvious first example of what the churches "stand behind" in our day. By what hocus-pocus of interpretation can these platforms of faith be presented as anything other than what they are – a record of controversies long since forgotten and of beliefs long since disproved? How can we expect modern man to express his spiritual ideals in such terms as that of Trinity or Atonement or even Revelation? We do not expect men to light their houses by candle, to travel in stagecoaches, to converse in Latin or to live in the thought-world of Plato. Why then should we expect them to articulate ideals in thought-patterns of the fourth and fifth centuries A.D.? Chroniclers might be interested in these documents, but not prophets. Antiquarians might lose sleep thinking about a credal statement, but a martyr will not lose blood over it. The church needs a handful of antiquarians and chroniclers. But it needs armies of prophets and martyrs.

It might be argued that the language of the church is, after all, a technical one, meant to be understood by a kind of professional technician – the minister-theologian. Perhaps this kind of argument was defensible in a day when most people could not read and when a priest served to mediate knowledge to the ill-informed masses. But today the language of theology has lost any mystique that it may have had for a past age. Ministers are just as baffled and offended as laymen at the sea of words that pours forth from weighty volumes of theology and liturgy. I have read widely in the field of Christian theology and I confess to you that I have cried out in exasperation time and time again: "But I cannot understand what you are saying!" I am appalled as I read of the modern insistence that we must move away from the Jesus of history and dwell on a "Christ of faith". Such a "Christ" is a creation of the church, and seems to many laymen and ministers alike as a kind of smoke-screen behind which to avoid coming to grips with the earthy and simple message of Jesus of Nazareth. In its increased sophistication the church is moving ever farther from its people. It moves toward the worship of a Being who is removed from life and cannot be understood, a Being unrooted to life-as-we-know-it, and who seems incapable of giving guidance to modern man's tortured search for meaning. Theology has become so ethereal that, in its dogmatic and creedal formulations at least, it is not understood by laymen and not accepted by science.

But churches are still full and memberships continue to climb. Does this mean that modern man can somehow accept dogmatic Christianity while still remaining modern? I do not think so. Rather he continues to patronize dogmatic religion because, from bill-boards to newspaper ads, he is urged to "attend the church of his choice," to be a part of some religious society – for his country's sake if for no other. By giving in to these pressures, and by forcing himself to be in his pew on Sunday morning, he is causing a serious self-deception. It is a self-deception understood by many psychiatrists who recognize a religious factor in many modern neuroses, but which is usually not recognized by the person himself. He continues to say "I believe" to the creeds although both his mind and his heart rebel at the words. What does this dishonesty do to him? It pulls him apart – into a kind of hypocrisy that is not his creation but the church's. How can he assert a belief in a Deity ruling over a Universe that science re-arranged centuries ago, a Universe that is not the one believed in today? How can he listen to a church that speaks of laying up treasures in heaven while so often it is laying up its own treasures upon earth?

The duplicity is not only within the personalities of many church people. It reaches out to society itself, particularly to the young. It is no secret to children and young people that most adults believe little of what the church teaches; but by the public display of faith adults convey a subtle "what difference does it make" attitude. Integrity is replaced by propriety. This is one exchange the young simply refuse to make. A quick scanning of a typical Sunday morning congregation will reveal how little the young are willing to make this exchange, for their absence is a loud cry to the church: FOR GOD'S SAKE, BE HONEST.

Yes, the churches are full. Budgets rise year by year. Membership rolls bulge. But they have ceased to be the moral and spiritual backbone of society if the typical pattern of churchmanship is a lip-service divorced from genuine belief. Indeed, the church may even be playing a negative role in the community – fostering a false sense of security and keeping alive an understanding of the universe and man's place in it, which makes of him a puny automaton. Certainly fewer and fewer men in our day will commit themselves in depth to a church that lives too much by double-talk and dogma. In private and occasionally in public, laymen and clergy are admitting their malaise about the church. It is weighed in the balance and found wanting.

What shall we say about the correlate of dogmatism: denominationalism? Why is the church, in 1969, still divided into over 270 different groupings – groupings based not on life differences but on articles of creed, ritual, and ecclesiastical order? If the church is really a Body that is a Unity for the achievement of human values, why do we have diverse and even rival churches? The question is asked so frequently today that it seems naive to mention it here. But let us not be put off by the church's inaction in the matter of dropping its denominational lines. Let us not even regard the ecumenical movement as a break from denominationalism, because it is essentially a movement of re-alignment, and awareness of one's denominational lines are often intensified instead of loosened. Witness the extreme care with which merging communions insist that their particular patterns are kept *alive* in the new grouping. In our day the church is still stuck in the groove of feeling that its expression in the world must be defensive of some article of truth or other. And as long as churches are defensive and retentionist, they will always be denominational.

The peculiar thing is that denominations are not grouped according to differences that are alive and significant in today's world. If this were so, denominationalism would still be wrong, but it would at least be understandable. How queer that in order to find out what is distinctive about the denominations one must consult a musty volume in a theological library. There one will discover that a hair-line distinction regarding God's nature or man's nature, or the political fortunes of this monarch or that bishop remain the essential lines of demarcation. A survey of world history since the Middle Ages will show how radically altered national boundaries have been (indeed this can be said of our century); but church boundaries remain as firm as they were centuries ago. The Berlin Wall is nothing compared to the wall of history and pride that has divided Christian churches. The continuing existence of denominational churches serves only to keep alive on the world stage controversies that should have been interred with the personalities who fomented them. The names that are applied to the churches themselves point to a past age and carry the odor of a gutted candle. Yet if the churches are challenged to deliver themselves from "the body of this death" – to prove the sincerity of their spiritual confessions by dropping their separate names, abandoning their competitiveness, burying their rancid disputations, and by uniting in a common cause in the name of God's Kingdom – they hesitate, and shamefully refuse. They will not throw down their denominational barriers and become as "one Body in Christ".

It is an interesting mental exercise to consider all the elements of the denominations that are *distinguishing marks* from other groups. List these as they come to your mind – denomination by denomination – and you will discover that all of them are at best fringe concerns, having nothing to do with the essentials of Christian faith. It would seem that the churches are more interested in the preservation of theological ideas than in Christian work – more interested in dogmas of the past than duties of the present and dreams of the future. Churches are denominational first, Christian second. They have the marks of a "Society for the Preservation of Old Dogma," but the church is called to be a "Society for the Announcement of New Things!"

But in the welter of archaic slogans how difficult it is to hear about the new things. If the essential message of Jesus came through or over the denominational defenses, then no great damage would be done. The fact is, however, that the average Sunday congregation hears little or nothing of the simple Good News that He announced. What more is there than the invitation: "Ye are my disciples if ye love one another"? Can we dispute the Golden Rule or play word-games with the Beatitudes? Here is Christianity – and here is no argument. If these could be agreed on by the churches and an end made of denominational wrangling, then how quickly the church would come into its own. During wartime, when a country finds new unity through the recognition of a few simple ideals like freedom and dedication, how rapidly religious differences evaporate away: Jew stands beside Presbyterian and neither asks the other whether they have a historical right to be shoulder-to-shoulder. The central message is still alive in the churches; but, it is so buried and lost beneath triviality that it is heard but faintly.

When Abraham Lincoln was asked about his religious opinions, and more especially about his attitude toward the various churches of Christendom, he replied, "I have never united myself to any church, because I have found difficulty in giving assent to the long, complicated statements of Christian doctrine, which characterize their articles of belief. . . . When any church will ascribe over its altar, as its sole qualification of membership, 'Thou shalt love the Lord thy God with all thy heart and with all thy soul and with all thy mind; and thy neighbour as thyself,' that church will I join with all my heart and soul." The great president was looking for a church that dealt exclusively with the essentials of religion – but he did not find one.

I believe there is a solution to the problem, and the clear words of Lincoln hold the secret. Why not such a church as he yearned for? Why not a church without denominational walls? Why not a church for the community?

A *Community* Church. The words ring. Our age cries out for a spiritual "home" in which men as men can feel they have a share, as men – and not as Baptists or Orthodox or Catholics. Religion is an instinct of the human spirit that cannot be locked within one "supreme expression". All men are religious in their innermost heart, and they seek to give expression to the impulses that move within them. The time of religious *difference* has been a creative period, and prophets and wise men from many backgrounds have each seen their own visions and dreamed their own dreams. But the time of local nationalisms and prejudices has ended in the post-war fact of One World. The United Nations is our hope for unity in a world in which nationalisms are strange throw-backs to a past century; surely this applies equally well to the various religions of the world. Can they not all be seen as integral parts of the sum total of human experience in the spirit? Christianity would take its place as *one* part of that whole, for at its best it is also an expression of the one spirit, determined by prophetic leadership, by historical accident, by intellectual revolutions and break-throughs, by great crises in the moral and social life. The same is true of Judaism, Buddhism, Islam – though each has discovered some fact about God undisclosed to the others. When the great parliament of religions gathered in Chicago in 1893 the world saw a promise of one religious unity in the world. Could it happen, men asked. I am certain that a Community Church could realize in a single fellowship and at a local level what was envisioned in that parliament. It seeks to take men not *out* of the community and its everyday concerns, but more deeply *into* the community. It could be the fulfilment of both social and spiritual needs.

What are some of the marks of a Community Church as I see it? It would clearly not be exclusively Christian. Instead of being faithful to the ideals (and historical core) of one religion, it would be faithful to the community as such. It would be a unity of spiritual integration for the community – and people from every religious "background" would be welcome without further tests of faith. For behind each "incarnation" of the truth – Buddha, Moses, Jesus – there is the same God, who is Love. Our unity would not be based on loyalty to the particular person in whom our tradition has placed supreme revelation, but rather to the common Reality beyond them all and to the common life that we have together. We would unite in love for God and for Man.

Furthermore, the Community Church would be a democratic church. The spiritual value of each person living in a community would be accepted and recognized. Just as a citizen in a community has rights that are common to all without the need for loyalty to anything but the community itself, so the community church would have as its membership everyone living in the community! And just as a citizen may or may not *exercise* all his rights, e.g., in the vote, so may he exercise his life in the church as he sees fit. The same holds true with respect to the particular style of the church in a given community. It would be a democratic place of exchange in worship and discussion in which each is able to teach as well as learn from the insights of every other member. It would be neither anti- nor pro-Christian, nor anti- nor pro-Jewish. The old labels would hang on for a while (just as Canadians hang on to European labels although their forefathers landed here three or four generations ago); but gradually they would drop away and the words "Christian" and "Buddhist" would be as quaint as the words "Norman" and "Saxon". The main fact about this kind of church would be that its altar would be so wide and beautiful that all men would come to it gladly. It would be (in the words of Jesus) "not to destroy but to fulfil".

As a Christian, I would not hesitate to be a part of such a

church. In fact, there is solid evidence that this is exactly what Jesus had in mind when he urged men to leave behind their differences that divided. He did not close the ranks of those who could or could not be disciples on the basis of their spiritual attainments. Instead he asked of them only good-will and the willingness to endure. It is impossible to see anything in His life or teaching to support any *other* kind of religious community than one with no barriers to membership. The word "Christian" was not even his invention or that of the disciples, and it could well be that Jesus had no intention of his group assuming a label and becoming yet another alternative to the many that the world had at that time. Certainly the Christian religion could enter into such a fellowship gladly, in confidence that it was only expressing the spirit of its founder. His own spirit was as wide as the circle of humanity and as deep as the depths of human woe. I am inclined to believe that a universal religion would really be the final and best development of the Christian religion, and that the Community Church would be the mark of this universality in a local setting. Who knows, this might well be the kind of brotherhood in the mind of all the great prophets; and it would come into reality in our age.

What kind of ministry will there be in such a church? My only feeling is one of optimism. It would be a free church with a free pulpit and a free pew. The people would understand that it is not necessary for minister and congregation to agree on everything. There would be an understanding that all must wrestle with life's questions and together try to come to some answers. There would be constant growth for all who entered into the life together with earnestness. No one would have decided ahead of time what the Truth is. I want to serve in a free church that has a prophetic and always-growing faith. I want to be part of a community group that would be unafraid to speak out on social problems and world peace.

CHAPTER 17

There is, of course, one aspect of my past work that must be a part of my future; I fully intend to work with delinquent youth. I must do this, despite the fact that it is these persons who co-operated to try to destroy me.

I have spent my very life for such youth in order to redirect their lives into more positive channels. All my ministry has centred on their needs, and I know no other challenge.

I am motivated now in this direction, as I always have been, in response to the great need for positive, intelligent programs for our young people. I have shown the appalling lack of community involvement in the lives of modern youth. They respond with a sense of futility, of alienation, of deep and pervasive boredom. For many, these sinister emotions lead directly to overt delinquency and rebellion. The church has a clear mandate to enter into the midst of this situation and to contribute its resources toward a solution of this problem. The church must not aim its efforts at conformity or outward adjustment among our youth to the expectations of society and parents; instead, it must be a partner with the young in the creation of lives that have meaning, direction or satisfaction. The need to move the church from its cloisters and into these mainstreams of community life is pressing, and I must contribute to the answering of this need.

Both these reasons have been life-long motivations within me that have led me to my past involvement with delinquent youth. I now find a third and dominant reason leads me back to this way of life again; a desire to make the legal difficulties of my recent past meaningful in my future.

I can think of no better way of doing this than by translating my frustrations, my humiliations, and my despair into a greater understanding of the lives that have been foisted upon the young. Most delinquent youths have little sympathy for the men and techniques of our legal system; I appreciate that fully. Most of them are plagued by thoughts of a marked or spoiled future; again, I have felt that. Most of them have made the serious efforts to find help and have been rejected coldly; that is a personal experience that I have encountered countless times. Most have felt, at some time, that all men must be evil or stupid, and that their society established rules designed simply to rob men of life's pleasure; I, too, have looked out at the world in this way and have despaired.

There are more positive experiences that I want to provide for these young people, just as they were given to me when I needed them. I have learned how deeply relieved a person can feel when he finds another person who will listen sympathetically. I know the depth of gratitude for the discovery of a friendship that has led me beyond the hopelessness of the present and into a greater perspective of my whole life. I have learned how happily small diversions can lift great portions of despair. I have met strangers who wanted nothing but the chance to be generous. These, and countless other events both large and small, have given me a new framework, a new set of guidelines for an understanding of young people with problems and a new desire to help them.

In the past, I found my work with young people to be personally enriching, and I still regard this work as the most effective that I have undertaken. As a result, I intend to pursue it again. I do not want my recent legal encounters to cripple my future. I intend, instead, to build upon them toward a more complete life.

It would seem very improbable that the Crown could now bring new charges against Mr. Horsburgh. The charges brought on June 29th, 1964 were withdrawn by the Crown on July 8th when amended charges were brought in and these were again withdrawn by the Crown when new information and reworded charges were substituted on July 15th. Now, the Court has told the Crown that even after three attempts the charges are still invalid.

On July 15th the Crown Attorney told the Court that he had no secrets in this matter and that he had no further details of time, place or subject matter which he could put in the charges. If this is correct, then the Crown does not have any facts on which to base a prima facie case or draw valid charges. If this is not correct and the Crown now brings charges setting out an offence with sufficient details as to time, place and subject matter so that the accused could know with what he is charged, the integrity of the Crown Attorney would be subject to serious question.

It would be very interesting to know why these invalid charges were brought or what influenced this distortion of the processes of law . . . . The whole matter has tarnished the reputation of the administration of justice in our County. . . .

– *excerpt from C. E. Perkins' statement made to the press in July, 1964, following the quashing of all charges brought against the Reverend Russell Horsburgh*

EPILOGUE

Courtrooms set the stage for subtle, bloodless wars. There, men join battle with all the blind fervor, slogans, and arguments of the commanding generals of opposing armies. They are struggling over the landscape of the accused person's history, intentions, and deeds. Their weapons are the precedents of the past, the laws of the present, the prejudices of their society, and the absolute certainty of their own position.

This is the condition of the adversaries. Two men, the Crown and the Defence counsels, strike a pose, present their case and give way to others only when forced. Blind justice – the jury and the judge – are most often required to seek the truth that rests between, and to balance this truth toward the presentation that most closely represents it.

In theory, this drama will eventually present one understandable truth. In theory, justice is blind. It hears only the arguments offered and has no prejudices, no outside pressures, no overriding handicaps. In fact, justice, like victory in a war, is dispensed to the strong, the wily, and the persuasive.

It is my contention that justice operates all too frequently under distorted conditions, and that men are brought to the courtroom without the benefit of even a minimum hope of survival.

Consider the strength of the Crown as it presents its case.

First of all, the Crown has had the resources of a powerful and wealthy government at its disposal. The police have devoted as many men as necessary to the investigation of the case. The specialists in the Attorney General's office have been available for whatever research and advice are needed for a successful courtroom appearance. Whatever financial burdens that this investigation and this research have entailed are absorbed by the budget of the Attorney General's office.

Secondly, it is the Crown's responsibility to prosecute a case, apparently not to seek for the enactment of a just trial against a specific man. The Crown is faced with two facts: a crime has been committed and a criminal must be convicted. If evidence merely points toward a man, that alone makes him guilty as far as the Crown is concerned. He may not, if justice is proven, actually be convicted. But, apparently, justice is not the concern of the Crown. Prosecution is its sole intention.

Thirdly, the Crown is often favored by the prejudices and the pressures of society at large. Newspaper reports affect jurymen. Judges are susceptible to our cultural assumptions. The procedures of our courts and the methods of appointing judges do not always guarantee that wise men sit on the Bench or that unbiased men serve on our juries.

Consider the strength of the Defence. One mighty weapon alone has saved our society of the burden of consistently condemning the innocent. The accused man is always innocent until proven guilty. The Crown must establish beyond a doubt that the accused has committed a crime and that he deserves the punishment of the law.

Against the strength of the police force, the legal experts, and the financial resources of the Crown, the Defence must fall back upon one man's income, and one lawyer's ability.

In my case, the Crown's strength caused me four years of legal harassment, three months imprisonment, and a lifetime of suspicions, prejudices, and difficulties. My only compensation, finally, was the restoration of my previous status as an innocent man.

Other writers have argued about the ways in which we can improve this imbalance in the dispensation of justice. In this text, I have given you a single case history, showing how I have been accused, convicted, imprisoned, and finally freed.

In summary, I want to show you the implications of improper justice for one man: myself.

Fourteen days in a Chatham courtroom have altered the pattern of my life irrevocably. These two weeks presented such lurid details under such widespread newspaper coverage that I shall bear their cost always. Four years later, in the same city, I was freed, legally; but I shall never be set free of the charges that were hurled at me with such reckless abandon by Chatham's Crown and police.

To defend myself, I was forced to draw on every financial resource at my disposal. My friends and supporters formed charitable committees and fund drives. The Board of Evangelism of the United Church provided me with a compassionate grant to alleviate my living expenses. My family made substantial gifts and loans. Even the banks adopted a more favorable attitude toward my habitual overdrafts. Despite such outside assistance, I was required to cash my pension funds, to empty my savings account, and to lower my standard of living to the borderline of abject poverty.

A few months after my conviction, I resigned from the Ministry of the United Church of Canada. I was at the peak of my career, serving in one of the largest congregations in Ontario, working at one of the most successful, active programs that I had yet accomplished. I had found that my ability to preach, to reach out through the Church's actions and my willingness to face new problems and challenges were matched by a growing sense of personal confidence and accomplishment. In Chatham, despite an occasionally stormy ministry, I found that I considered myself most satisfied with my career and most eager to continue its development.

After my resignation, I dropped to the pit of my life's course. I became a beggar, living off the gifts and jobs that others made available. I worked in a parking lot; I filed cards in the basement of a publishing company's offices. Employment agencies told me that few firms would even consider hiring a condemned man.

Since my retrial, I have embarked on an adventure in creating a social service agency to handle juvenile delinquents. Constantly I am told that I am unfit for the work, that I am in a shaky career or that I should not persevere in the very area where I encountered such problems. I have been refused re-admission to the church I had served all my life. It will undoubtedly be a long and terrible road back to the peaks I once enjoyed.

Far more sweeping in its destructiveness, however, than all these events is the scorn that constantly faces me. I am an innocent man, but I am far from free. Continuously, I meet other people who think that I have escaped justice merely through smart tactics. I am forced to overcome lingering prejudices and hidden suspicions. Whenever I appear in person or in conversations, eyebrows lift and doubts arise. It is questionable that I shall ever appear again in an active life as an ordained clergyman.

Condemning the innocent is an easy and prevalent habit. Although history may occasionally find room for a grand case, a Captain Dreyfus, and may set such men as martyrs and warning signs, most condemned innocents slide away to new lives as modern outcasts. They become untouchables. The mere fact of accusation, without a conviction, may mar terribly a man's future. His work, income, friendships, and personal satisfactions may slip into despairing depths.

I am now aware that I must build anew the pattern of my own life. I have written this book to show the raw materials of a legal decision, to show the extent to which the cogs of a great social machine may catch and destroy.

But I have written this book, also, to show that my faith in the ultimate triumph of good over evil has not been shattered. I believe, more than ever, that God has placed within the very structure of the universe certain absolute moral laws. We can neither defy nor break them. If we disobey them, they will break us. The forces of evil and injustice may temporarily conquer truth; but truth will ultimately conquer its conqueror. James Russell was right:

Truth forever on the scaffold, Wrong forever on the throne,–
Yet that scaffold sways the future, and behind the dim unknown,
Standeth God within the shadow, keeping watch above His own.